*American
Quilts & Coverlets*

American Quilts & Coverlets in The Metropolitan Museum of Art

by Amelia Peck

THE METROPOLITAN MUSEUM OF ART, NEW YORK

&

DUTTON STUDIO BOOKS, NEW YORK

This volume has been published in conjunction with the exhibition
American Quilts & Coverlets in The Metropolitan Museum of Art,
held at The Metropolitan Museum of Art from October 16, 1990, through
January 20, 1991.

The exhibition was made possible by Dr. and Mrs. Burton P. Fabricand
and Mr. and Mrs. Edward J. Scheider.

This publication has been made possible in part by the William Cullen
Bryant Fellows of The American Wing, The Metropolitan Museum of Art.

Published by The Metropolitan Museum of Art, New York, and
Dutton Studio Books, New York

John P. O'Neill, *Editor in Chief*
Barbara Burn, *Project Supervisor*
Barbara Cavaliere, *Editor*
Joseph B. Del Valle, *Designer*
Matthew Pimm, *Production*

Dutton Studio Books
Published by the Penguin Group
Penguin Books USA Inc., 375 Hudson Street, New York, New York, U.S.A. 10014
Penguin Books Ltd, 27 Wrights Lane, London W8 5TZ, England
Penguin Books Australia Ltd, Ringwood, Victoria, Australia
Penguin Books Canada, 2801 John Street, Markham, Ontario, Canada L3R 1B4
Penguin Books (N.Z.) Ltd., 182-190 Wairau Road, Auckland 10, New Zealand

Penguin Books Ltd, Registered Offices: Harmondsworth, Middlesex, England

First printing, October 1990
10 9 8 7 6 5 4 3 2 1

Library of Congress Cataloging-in-Publication Data
Peck, Amelia.
    American quilts & coverlets in the metropolitan museum of art/by
Amelia Peck.
        p.   cm.
    Includes bibliographical references.
    ISBN 0-87099-592-8—ISBN 0-525-24912-5 (Dutton Studio Books)
    1. Quilts—United States—Catalogs. 2. Quilts—New York (N.Y.)—
Catalogs. 3. Coverlets—United States—Catalogs. 4. Coverlets—New York
(N.Y.)—Catalogs. 5. Metropolitan Museum of Art (New York, N.Y.)—
Catalogs. I. Metropolitan Museum of Art (New York, N.Y.) II. Title. III.
Title: American quilts and coverlets in the Metropolitan Museum of Art.
NK9112.P434   1990
746.9'7'09730747471—dc20   90-35929
                                                                  CIP

The photographs in this volume were taken by John Bigelow Taylor and by
The Photograph Studio, The Metropolitan Museum of Art.

Type set by U.S. Lithograph, typographers, New York
Printed and bound by Dai Nippon Printing Co., Ltd., Tokyo, Japan

Jacket front: Detail of Amish Pinwheel Quilt (catalogue no. 30)

Contents

Foreword

The publication of this catalogue of the American quilts and coverlets in The Metropolitan Museum of Art's collection is part of the Museum's ongoing mission to publish all aspects of its permanent collection in order to make these works of art more readily accessible to the public. Catalogues like this one are especially important because they provide the reader with information about a collection that, due to the fragile nature of textile fibers, is rarely exhibited. Every American bed cover in our collection has been photographed (more than half in color) for the book, and each piece is accompanied by complete information about its manufacture, materials, size, condition, and history. Our textile collection is an important part of our American decorative arts collection, and our holdings in quilts and coverlets are particularly strong. We are pleased to publish this book, knowing that it will be enjoyed by collectors and makers of quilts and coverlets as well as by all readers interested in the study of American decorative arts.

Philippe de Montebello
Director
The Metropolitan Museum of Art

Acknowledgments

W hen, in the fall of 1987, I first proposed writing a catalogue of The Metropolitan Museum of Art's collection of American quilts and coverlets, I had no idea how many people would contribute to the project's realization. First, I must thank the Museum's Director, Philippe de Montebello, for approving the catalogue. Mahrukh Tarapor, Assistant Director, and Linda M. Sylling, Assistant Manager for Operations, made many helpful suggestions regarding the exhibition accompanying the book's publication. That exhibition was made possible by the generous contributions of Dr. and Mrs. Burton P. Fabricand and Mr. and Mrs. Edward J. Scheider.

In the American Wing, my thanks go to the William Cullen Bryant Fellows, who committed funds to offset the costs of the color photography. John K. Howat, The Lawrence A. Fleischman Chairman of the Departments of American Art, always supported the project wholeheartedly. The day-to-day encouragement I received from Morrison H. Heckscher, Curator of American Decorative Arts, was essential to the successful completion of the book and the exhibition. Peter Kenny, Assistant Curator and Assistant for Administration, and his assistant, Emely Bramson, helped me through many administrative complications. I thank Alice Cooney Frelinghuysen, Associate Curator, Frances Gruber Safford, Associate Curator, and Frances Bretter, Research Consultant, in the American Decorative Arts Department, and Kevin Avery, Assistant Curator, Carrie Rebora, Assistant Curator, Donna Hassler, Curatorial Assistant, and Dale Johnson, Research Consultant, in the American Paintings Department, for their friendship, and for listening to me go on when the going got tough. Outstandingly good natured as usual, our departmental technicians Don E. Templeton, Gary Burnett, and Edward Di Farnecio, put up with a lot, including freezing cold temperatures and the biggest easel in creation. Without the always able Ellin Rosenzweig and Seraphine Wu, Administrative Assistants, I would have never completed this book or mastered the computer system. Research Assistant Sarah Vure helped get the book started, and the enthusiastic efforts of American Wing volunteers Heather Fabricand, Madeline Farnsworth, and Elizabeth Quackenbush are greatly appreciated.

The American Wing had many talented textile curators in the past; I would like to acknowledge Marilynn Johnson, whose astute eye enriched our quilt collection so significantly during the 1970s, and the late Oswaldo Rodriguez Roque, who taught me many essential lessons about both art and life.

The Museum's Editorial Department was invaluable in all stages of the book's publication. Barbara Burn, Executive Editor, was excited about the book from the very beginning, and Barbara Cavaliere edited it with a sharp eye and consistent good humor. Ruth Kozodoy got the initial editing off the ground, and Mary Smith prepared the disks for the typesetter with speed and accuracy. The book's designer, Joseph B. Del Valle, and Production Associate Matthew Pimm made it beautiful. John Bigelow Taylor, ably assisted by Steven J. Titus, took wonderful pictures.

I would also like to thank the Metropolitan's superb Textile Conservation Department, headed by Nobuko Kajitani. Elena Phipps, Associate Conservator, was always helpful, and Cristina B. Carr, Conservation Assistant, contributed to the project in innumerable ways, both concrete and intangible. Alice Zrebiec, Associate Curator in Charge of the Textile Study Room, was always interested in the book's progress. Without R. Craig Miller, Associate Curator in the Twentieth Century Art Department, I would never have come to the Museum, and I am grateful for his friendship over the past ten years. Archivist Jeanie James and her staff patiently answered my questions about provenances. Barbara Bridgers, Manager of the Photo Studio, generously helped with rush photo orders.

Many curators and historians at other institutions have given me pertinent information and ideas. I extend my gratitude to Diane L. Fagan Affleck, Curator of Textiles, Museum of American Textile History; Gloria Seaman Allen, Director and Chief Curator, Daughters of the American Revolution Museum; Phyllis Barr, Archivist, Parish of Trinity Church; Russell Bastedo, Director, The Stamford Historical Society; Lisa L. Broberg, Curator, The Wethersfield Historical Society; Sandi Fox, Senior Research Associate, American Quilt Research Center, Los Angeles County Museum of Art; Nina Gray, Associate Curator, The New-York Historical Society; Frank L. Horton, Director Emeritus, Museum of Early Southern Decorative Arts; Dena S. Katzenberg, Consultant Curator of Textiles, The Baltimore Museum of Art; James R. Lynch, Director of the Library, American Baptist Historical Society; Kristan McKinsey, Curatorial Assistant, The Saint Louis Art Museum; Gillian Moss, Associate Curator, The Cooper-Hewitt Museum; Christopher B. Nevins, Curator, The Fairfield Historical Society; Eileen J. O'Brien, Special Collections Librarian, New York State Historical Association; Maurice L. Patterson, Historian, Town of Covert, New York; Katharine P. Randall, Genealogical Researcher, Bergen County Historical Society; Ann Pollard Rowe, Curator, New World Textiles, The Textile Museum; Alesandra M. Schmidt, Head, References Services, The Connecticut Historical Society; Marjorie D. Smith, Historian, Town of Thompson, New York; Richard J. Sommers, Ph.D., Archivist-Historian, U.S. Army Military History Institute; Professor Ed Sullivan, Curator of the J. Doyle DeWitt Collection, University of Hartford; Susan Burrows Swan, Curator and in Charge of Textiles, Winterthur Museum; Neil Todd, New England Historic Genealogical Society; Elsie Winterberger, Historian, Town of Forestburgh, New York; Kevin Wright, Curator, Steuben House. Also unfailingly generous with their time and knowledge were: Sandra S. Armentrout, Robert W. Barnes, Cuesta Benberry, Katherine C. Grier, Patricia Herr, Roderick Kiracofe, Joel and Kate Kopp, Frank D. McNeil, Florence Montgomery, and Stella Rubin.

Finally, I am grateful to my family, all of the Pecks, Grobsmiths, and Altshulers who, over the course of the past thirty-four years, have both challenged and supported me every step of the way. This book is dedicated to Michael and Annie, with love.

Amelia Peck
Assistant Curator, Department of American Decorative Arts
The Metropolitan Museum of Art

Introduction

The Metropolitan Museum of Art's collection of American quilts and coverlets is extremely diverse, encompassing excellent representative examples of most types of bed coverings. Bed covers from many regions of the United States are included, but our collection is strongest in works from the Middle Atlantic and New England states, since we are an East Coast institution that during the earlier decades of this century acquired bed coverings primarily as gifts and bequests from local families. As might be expected, the collection has grown in accordance with trends in twentieth-century connoisseurship of American decorative arts. A number of the bed covers acquired by the Museum during the decades before World War II were valued primarily for the historical importance of either their makers or their original owners rather than for the beauty or significance of the objects themselves. This approach pervaded many areas of antiques collecting beginning with the nation's Centennial in 1876, when a newly awakened interest in our country's colonial past inspired many families to reevaluate their heirlooms. Many of the first quilts and coverlets to enter the Museum's collection were donated as part of a group of family treasures. For instance, one of our finest examples, a Honeycomb quilt made in New York City by Elizabeth Van Horne Clarkson in about 1830 (catalogue no. 3), was part of a large lot of objects given by Mr. and Mrs. William A. Moore, whose ancestors included the Schuylers and the Van Cortlandts, both prominent early American families from the Hudson River Valley in New York State. In addition to the one quilt, this gift also included miniature paintings of family members, silver, furniture, and ephemera. Our early nineteenth-century woven counterpane (catalogue no. 48) came to the Museum along with an embroidered wedding gown from the same period that was worn by the donor's great aunt, another New Yorker of long standing. Some quilts and coverlets were purchased by the Museum during the early decades of the twentieth century; very often the overriding reason for their purchase was their history of ownership by a person or family known to have been prominent in colonial America.

By the 1940s, quiltmaking was being reassessed, and some collectors began to regard it as a fine art form in its own right. This reconsideration surely influenced the decision to purchase our 1945 crib quilt (catalogue no. 36), which was added to the collection because it illustrated the rising popularity of quiltmaking as an artistic endeavor. By the late 1960s and early 1970s, the idea of collecting quilts and coverlets for their genealogical value alone was almost entirely a thing of the past. This was the era of appreciation of the quilt as graphic art: The overall visual image of the quilt when it is hung on a wall is what collectors came to value most. Quilt collecting became acceptable, even fashionable. Amish quilts, newly discovered by the art community, were especially prized for the abstract compositions formed by their traditional geometric patterns and for their saturated colors. Amish quilt designs could easily be compared with paintings by modern masters such as Josef Albers and Piet Mondrian. Like many other collections, the Metropolitan acquired most of its Amish quilts in the early 1970s.

The 1980s saw the flowering of a scholarly methodology for the study of quilts and coverlets. Even while attention to the historical and purely aesthetic values of these objects continued, new considerations were also explored. Questions were asked to help broaden the scope of knowledge in the field. What roles did bed coverings of various types play in the lives of the women who made and owned them? Do works produced in the same region share distinctive characteristics, and, if so, how can these be described? What weaving or sewing technologies were available at various times? How did technological advances influence the look of bed coverings and the prevalence of one kind or another? At the start of the 1990s, all of these issues inform any serious investigation into the history of a quilt or coverlet, and with the continuing growth of the field, new subjects for study will inevitably arise.

Since 1910, when the Museum's first American bed covering was acquired, curators in the American Wing have gradually amassed an admirable collection. Except for a few justly famous pieces, however, it is largely unknown. The textile collections of many museums remain underexplored for several reasons. Traditionally, art museums have not emphasized the utilitarian, primarily homemade, and often anonymous items in their collections such as quilts. Additionally, bed coverings are difficult to exhibit because of their large size. Most importantly, because the cotton and silk textiles that make up many of these works are exceedingly fragile, a museum must take its job as cultural caretaker particularly seriously; by rarely displaying our bed covers, we are prolonging their lives. Over the years an increasing number of collectors, quiltmakers, coverlet weavers, scholars, and textile enthusiasts have asked to see our quilts and coverlets. The Museum staff is not able to accommodate requests to see the entire collection of 119 bed coverings. Only by prearrangement can we show a small number of them to an occasional viewer or allow visitors to make use of the catalogued information kept for study purposes. This book provides greater access to the Museum's outstanding collection and enables all who are interested to discover the beauty and historical significance of our American quilts and coverlets.

John K. Howat
The Lawrence A. Fleischman Chairman
of the Departments of American Art
The Metropolitan Museum of Art

American
Quilts & Coverlets

Highlights of the Collection

1. Phebe Warner Coverlet

Probably Sarah Furman Warner Williams
New York City, about 1803
Linen and cotton
Gift of Catharine E. Cotheal, 1938 (38.59)

This bed cover is perhaps the finest existing example of an American appliquéd coverlet. The work was made for Phebe Warner of New York in about 1803, and its design inevitably relates more closely to eighteenth-century sources than to those from the nineteenth century. Its maker was clearly influenced by the central flowering-tree motif common to the popular imported Indian bed hangings called palampores, as well as by the pastoral landscape needlework pictures often worked by young women during the eighteenth century. Like the maker of the Phebe Warner coverlet, the artist who made the needlework picture illustrated here (Figure 1) had a charming disregard for accurate scale and enjoyed decorating her work with a mixture of fantastical flora and fauna.

The Phebe Warner coverlet is decorated with pieces of cloth cut from both large-patterned chintzes and printed linens as well as with smaller-patterned cotton calicos and plaids. Most of these fabrics were manufactured in England. The pieces that are figures cut from chintz, such as the birds that peer down on the scene beneath them, are applied, or stitched down, with a nearly invisible whipstitch. Many of the pieces that were cut from the small-patterned fabrics are embroidered around their edges with silk thread in the buttonhole stitch. Some of the flowers in the border are formed from seven small hexagons of fabric, a very early use of a piecing style that remained popular for the next 150 years.

Figure 1. Needlework picture. Maker unknown, American, about 1750. Wool and silk on linen, 10¾ × 13¾ in. The Metropolitan Museum of Art, Gift of Mrs. Screven Lorillard, 1953 (53.179.13)

For many years, the Phebe Warner coverlet has been attributed to Phebe's mother, Ann Walgrove Warner (1758–1826). New evidence, however, points to its reattribution to another member of the family. Several additional pieces of appliquéd work from the Warner family are in the collections of other museums. Strikingly similar to our coverlet in style and craftsmanship, they were undoubtedly all made by the same person. The group includes two scenic panels in the collection of The Henry Francis du Pont Winterthur Museum, Delaware, each meant to be set into the center of a coverlet like ours: a nativity scene, 33½ inches square, from about 1805 (acc. no. 59.1496), and a rendering of the Holy Family's Flight into Egypt, 40⅝ x 40¾ inches, from about 1810–30 (acc. no. 59.1497). Both these panels are attributed to Sarah Furman Warner Williams of New York City.

Also obviously sewn by the same hand are the remains of a coverlet, shown here (Figure 2) as it appeared before 1970, when it was damaged in a fire at The Henry Ford Museum and Greenfield Village, Dearborn, Michigan. It too is traditionally regarded as the work of Sarah Furman Warner Williams. This attribution is supported by documents that descended through the Nichols family of Greenfield Hill, Connecticut, and are now owned by the Fairfield Historical Society. One handwritten note relates that the Henry Ford coverlet was made for Susannah Nexsen Warner, who married the Reverend Samuel Nichols of Greenfield Hill, and that it was marked in cross-stitch with the initials "S.N.W." According to another note, the coverlet, called "Aunt Williams Quilt," was exhibited in Fairfield, and there is "another at Met. Museum of Art."

Sarah Furman Warner Williams was born in the 1760s. Her mother was Magdelen Walgrove Warner, and her stepfather was George Warner, a sailmaker. The Winterthur Museum owns a pastel portrait of Sarah (Figure 3), probably drawn when she was in her teens. She married Azriah Williams in December 1783; we have not found any records of children born to the couple. The two surviving completed coverlets she made were sewn for younger relatives, perhaps as wedding gifts. Susannah Nexsen Warner Nichols was Sarah's niece, the child of her half brother, George James Warner (1774–1810). Susannah (1799–1880) married in 1816, which seems a likely date for the manufacture of The Henry Ford Museum's coverlet.

Phebe Berrien Warner Cotheal, the original owner of the Metropolitan's coverlet, was Sarah's first cousin. Phebe, at least twenty years younger than Sarah, was born in 1786, three years after Sarah was married. She was the only child of Ann Walgrove Warner and Charles Warner (1755–1811). On October 17, 1803, at the age of seventeen, Phebe married Henry Cotheal, a New York City merchant; the couple had a son and two daughters. After her death in 1844, the coverlet apparently descended to her son, Alexander Isaac Cotheal (1804–1892), and then to his daughter, Catharine Cotheal, who donated it to the Museum. Catharine Cotheal described it as the work of her great-grandmother Ann Walgrove Warner, but all the evidence indicates that it was made by her grandmother's cousin Sarah.

Genealogical research is particularly satisfying when it succeeds in clarifying the origins of an extraordinary work of art. The Phebe Warner coverlet and all the appliquéd work made by Sarah Furman Warner Williams are of a quality rarely seen in early nineteenth-century American textiles. The woman who made them possessed a keenly original imagination and was a craftsperson of the highest order. The design on this masterful coverlet delights us with its disregard for realistic scale: The couple continues to court, and the children to play, under the benevolent gaze of brightly plumed birds three times human size, while deer cavort among dogs, sheep, and pigs in the shadow of an urn the size of a house.

Figure 3. Portrait of Sarah Furman Warner Williams. William J. Williams, 1781. Pastel on paper, 20 1/16 × 14½ in. Courtesy, The Henry Francis du Pont Winterthur Museum, Winterthur, Delaware

Opposite
Figure 2. Coverlet made for Susannah Nexsen Warner. Sarah Furman Warner Williams, New York City, about 1816. Damaged in a fire in 1970 at The Henry Ford Museum. Courtesy, The Henry Ford Museum and Greenfield Village, Dearborn, Michigan

2. Chintz Appliquéd Quilt

Mary Malvina Cook Taft (1812–?)
Possibly Maryland, Virginia, or South Carolina, about 1830–35
Cotton
Gift of Miss Elsey R. Taft, 1970 (1970.288)

Like the Phebe Warner coverlet (catalogue no. 1), this quilt is appliquéd with pieces of chintz to form a Tree of Life motif at its center. This design strongly recalls that of Indian palampores, painted and dyed single-panel Indian cotton bed hangings that are often decorated with a central flowering tree. Chintz appliquéd quilts such as this one, sometimes called Broderie Perse quilts, were very popular in the South during the first half of the nineteenth century. In the late nineteenth century, the name Broderie Perse (French for "Persian embroidery") was given to appliqué work in which design elements such as birds and flowers were cut from printed fabrics and sewn onto a new background. The appliquéd pieces were often fastened down with blind whipstitch, but in some examples, more decorative buttonhole stitching was used. Because Broderie Perse is not a term contemporary with the actual quilts, this book refers to this type of quilt as chintz appliquéd. According to family history, Mary Malvina Cook Taft made our quilt for her trousseau. She was born in 1812, and assuming that she was married by her early twenties as was customary during this period, the quilt was probably made sometime between 1830 and 1835. There is no documentation of where the piece was made, but stylistically, it seems most closely related to documented bed covers from Maryland, Virginia, and South Carolina. It is a fairly late example of the chintz appliquéd style, which by 1840 was losing popularity in favor of the pieced quilt.

The English chintzes used for the appliqués on this quilt illustrate the appealingly vigorous quality of mid-nineteenth-century textile designs. The central tree is constructed from pieces of chintz showing vibrant pink roses in full bloom. The "basket" in which the tree is planted was cut from an English pillar print of about 1830–35, on which the column capitals overflow with a variety of boldly drawn flowers. The rather more modest palm trees that decorate the outer border can be traced to another English chintz, which was probably manufactured in about 1812. Either this fabric continued to be available well into the nineteenth century or for many years the maker's family carefully saved scraps of chintz left over from furniture and curtains.

3.   Honeycomb Quilt

Elizabeth Van Horne Clarkson (1771–1852)
New York City, about 1830
Cotton
Gift of Mr. and Mrs. William A. Moore, 1923 (23.80.75)

Elizabeth Van Horne Clarkson made this extraordinary quilt from hundreds of small hexagonal pieces of fabric. Outstanding in both intricacy of design and skilled needlework, it is the earliest wholly pieced American quilt in the Museum's collection.

Although pieced quilts were popular in England beginning in the eighteenth century, the technique, with a few rare exceptions, did not catch on in America until the nineteenth century. The proliferation of cottons printed with small-scale designs in the early decades of the nineteenth century may have stimulated more interest in the technique, perhaps because of the sampler-like aspects of a pieced quilt. Increased leisure time made quiltmaking more popular, and both domestic and imported printed cottons were considerably less expensive to work with than fine English chintzes, such as those used in the Phebe Warner coverlet (catalogue no. 1).

Elizabeth Van Horne Clarkson's quilt was made in the pattern known in the early decades of the nineteenth century as Honeycomb, in which each tiny hexagon of fabric was first formed over a template cut out of stiff paper in the same shape. Hexagon quilts are built up from small to larger units. After each individual cloth hexagon has been shaped around a hexagonal piece of paper backing, seven of these are whipstitched together to make a schematic flower: six hexagons for the petals, one for the flower's center. It is a technique that requires a patient needleworker. By designing a large and elaborate central medallion and a carefully pieced border, Elizabeth Clarkson elevated this common, methodical technique to create a quilt of great beauty. The quilt's overall design preserves a continuity with earlier appliquéd quilts, which were also focused around a central motif; at the same time, it heralds the transition to a new quiltmaking style in which piecing, rather than appliquéing, would be the favored mode.

The following instructions from *Godey's Lady's Book* for mastering this extremely time-consuming method of quiltmaking appeared in the January 1835 issue (p. 41):

> Perhaps there is no patch-work that is prettier or more ingenious than the hexagon, or six-sided; this is also called honeycomb patch-work. To make it properly you must first cut out a piece of pasteboard of the size you intend to make the patches, and of a hexagon or six-sided form. Then lay this model on your calico, and cut your patches of the same shape, allowing them a little larger all round for turning in at the edges.
>
> Of course the patches must be all exactly of the same size. Get some stiff papers (old copy-books or letters will do) and cut them also into hexagons precisely the size of the pasteboard model. Prepare as many of these papers as you have patches. Baste or tack a patch upon every paper, turning down the edge of the calico over the wrong side.

Figure 4. Portrait miniature of Elizabeth Van Horne Clarkson. Thomas Seir Cummings (1804–1894), New York City, about 1844. Watercolor on ivory, 3⅞ × 3 in. The Metropolitan Museum of Art, Gift of Mr. and Mrs. William A. Moore, 1923 (23.80.83)

Sew together neatly over the edge, six of these patches, so as to form a ring. Then sew together six more in the same manner, and so on till you have enough. Let each ring consist of the same sort of calico, or at least of the same colour. For instance, one ring may be blue, another pink, a third yellow, &c. The papers must be left in, to keep the patches in shape till the whole is completed.

The daughter of Augustus Vallete Van Horne and Anna Van Cortlandt Marston Van Horne, Elizabeth Van Horne Clarkson was related to many important old New York families. On October 30, 1790, at the age of nineteen, she married Thomas Streatfeild Clarkson (1763–1844) of Flatbush, whose brother General Matthew Clarkson was a well-known Revolutionary War hero. Elizabeth's brother, Garrit Van Horne, was married to her husband's sister, Ann Margaret Clarkson. The couples built two neighboring houses at 31 and 33 Broadway in lower Manhattan.

Elizabeth's husband, who went by the name of Streatfeild, together with his brother Levinus, owned a prosperous import and export business called S. & L. Clarkson Company, which was based in New York City. Perhaps this business supplied Elizabeth with the English cottons that she pieced into her quilt. After Streatfeild's death in 1844, Elizabeth moved to 11 West Twenty-first Street, where she died in 1852 at the age of eighty-two. She and her husband were interred in the Clarkson family vault in Flatbush.

The couple had eleven children, nine daughters and two sons. Elizabeth Clarkson's quilt apparently descended to her son Thomas Streatfeild Clarkson (1799–1873), who in 1828 married his first cousin Elizabeth Clarkson (1810–1883), Levinus's daughter. (As with many well-to-do families at the time, the Clarkson and Van Horne families continually intermarried, most likely in order to keep their wealth intact.) From them, the piece descended to the donors, Elizabeth's great-granddaughter and her husband, who in 1923 presented it to the Museum along with a large store of other family articles. The only quilt in the lot, it was obviously a valued heirloom.

It is tempting to suppose that Elizabeth made the quilt as a wedding present for her son Thomas. If completed in 1828, it is a very early example of this type of template quilt in America, although hexagon quilts were made in England beginning in about 1780. It is possible that through her husband's import/export contacts, Elizabeth learned about the popular English style before most of her compatriots. The first known publication in the United States of a pattern for hexagon patchwork was in the January 1835 issue of *Godey's Lady's Book* quoted above. The fabrics used in this quilt, all very well printed, were made in the first few decades of the nineteenth century; the latest of them has previously been dated to the early 1830s. Therefore, for the present, about 1830 must be considered the most accurate date we can assign to this work.

The Metropolitan Museum is fortunate to own, in addition to her quilt, a portrait miniature of Mrs. Clarkson (Figure 4). It was painted by New York miniaturist Thomas Seir Cummings (1804–1894) and depicts Mrs. Clarkson in her old age. Since she is shown dressed in black, the portrait was probably painted after the death of her husband in 1844.

Detail of catalogue no. 3

4

4. Honeycomb Quilt

Rebecca Davis
United States, 1846
Cotton
Gift of Mrs. Andrew Galbraith Carey, 1980 (1980.498.1)

5. Nine Patch Quilt

Rebecca Davis
United States, about 1846
Cotton
Gift of Mrs. Andrew Galbraith Carey, 1980 (1980.498.2)

6. Star of Lemoyne Quilt

Rebecca Davis
United States, about 1846
Cotton
Gift of Mrs. Andrew Galbraith Carey, 1980 (1980.498.3)

These three quilts were made by Rebecca Davis, grandmother of the donor, Mrs. Andrew Galbraith Carey. The Honeycomb or hexagon quilt (catalogue no. 4) is signed in the center of the schematic flower at the far right, second row from the bottom. The inscription, handwritten in black ink, reads: *Rebecca Davis/ 1846/March*. Although the other two quilts are not signed, we can assume that they were also made sometime around 1846, since all three share some of the same fabrics.

Most of the fabrics sewn into these quilts appear to be English printed cottons, an attribution confirmed by the sections of English design registration marks visible on a number of the pieces. The most complete mark identifies its fabric as having been registered in 1844. It is found on a lavender cotton pieced into the quilt with star-shaped figures (catalogue no. 6), a design known as Star of Lemoyne. Some of the pieces in the hexagon quilt are vividly colored rainbow prints, a type of fabric that gained great popularity in the 1840s. Its rainbow-like appearance is due to a special process used to spread the dye of the ground color in stripes that shade from light to dark.

Rebecca Davis had an excellent sense of color and design, especially noticeable in her Nine Patch quilt (catalogue no. 5). Although this quilt was probably the easiest to piece of the three and is certainly the most simply quilted, its pattern of internal symmetry is particularly attractive. The pattern has a focal point in the centermost square of the center block, which is flanked in all directions by pairs of matching blocks. Only the two outermost rows of blocks do not match, perhaps because Davis ran out of fabric.

Of these three quilts, only the one with the Star of Lemoyne pattern does not have a central focus. In the other two, the centralized design is subtle when compared with that of the Clarkson Honeycomb quilt made more than a decade earlier (catalogue no. 3). This illustrates the mid-nineteenth-century change of fashion from the pieced quilt with a strong central motif to the repeating block format that is still the most popular quiltmaking method today.

5

6

7. Star of Bethlehem Quilt

Maker unknown
Possibly Maryland, about 1835
Cotton
Sansbury-Mills Fund, 1973 (1973.204)

Although the provenance of this exquisite Star of Bethlehem quilt is not known, it was most likely made in one of the southern states. Quilts in which a central Star of Bethlehem motif is combined with chintz appliquéd blocks and a chintz border, as it is here, have been found in Maryland, Virginia, and North and South Carolina. It is tempting to conclude that this quilt originated in Maryland. For one thing, it exemplifies the very fine workmanship characteristic of the tradition of high-style quiltmaking that arose in Baltimore in the 1820s and reached its zenith with the famous Album quilts of the 1840s. A more fanciful reason for a Maryland attribution is the presence of Baltimore orioles on the four corner blocks, which are appliquéd with an English chintz printed with pairs of these birds. According to Florence Montgomery's *Printed Textiles*, between 1830 and 1834 an English manufacturer printed six chintz patterns incorporating plates from Audubon's *Birds of America*. These proved so popular that the fashion for bird prints was picked up by other designers. Montgomery believes that in the period between 1835 and 1840, one fabric designer specialized in prints of brightly colored birds common to North America (but not copied from Audubon): A bluejay print that seems to be from the same hand survives in addition to the Baltimore oriole chintz. These two fabrics are of good quality, although they do not match the beauty of the Audubon chintz designs. When this quilt was made, the American market was still dependent on England for well-printed chintzes, and naturally, American birds pleased the American buyer. The fabrics of this quilt's appliqués and border are English, while the printed cottons pieced into the central star are most likely of American manufacture. There is no quilting at all in the pieced star. The rest of the surface is worked with particularly fine, even quilting, and the white areas are enlivened with ten-pointed stuffed-work stars.

More than ten-feet square, this quilt is the largest in our collection. During the 1830s and 1840s, it was not unusual for quilts to be made this size and even larger. What was the purpose of such enormous quilts? This one was most likely a show quilt, meant to be displayed on special occasions to prove the skills of its maker; it looks almost unused and was never washed. However, very large quilts that clearly show wear exist from this period. In all likelihood, they were made to cover beds heaped high with piles of feather mattresses or straw ticks. Changes in the construction of mattresses may explain why quilts grew smaller as the nineteenth century progressed, until after about 1850, quilts nine- and ten-feet square were a rarity.

8.   Star of Bethlehem Quilt

Maker unknown
Possibly New York State, about 1845
Cotton
Purchase, Mr. and Mrs. Samuel Schwartz Gift, 1973 (1973.64)

This unusual quilt illustrates the transition that took place in the mid-nine-teenth century, when repeating block patterns began to take precedence over centrally focused quilt designs. While the large Star of Bethlehem motif in the middle remains the principal focus, the use of blocks with smaller stars in the border signals the approach of the new style. Quilts worked in blocks gained popularity over those with large centralized designs for a variety of reasons. One highly probable factor is that blocks of about twelve-inches square or smaller, because they are easily transportable, made it possible for women to work on a section of their quilt while visiting with friends. Although leisure time was on the rise in nineteenth-century America, a woman was still expected to fill most of her hours with some type of work that benefited her family, and the suppos-edly nonproductive activity of friendly visiting became acceptable when ac-companied by sewing. (For a fascinating description of the relationship between sewing and visiting, see Amy Boyce Osaki's 1988 article, "A 'Truly Feminine Employment.'")

Another possible reason for the ascendancy of pieced block patterns over appliquéd designs, which often depended on English chintzes for their deco-ration, stems from the rise of the printed cotton industry in the United States. By the 1830s, colorful printed cottons made in America were widely available, quite inexpensively and in great variety. In 1836, American mills manufactured some 120 million yards of these fabrics. Traditionally, it has been thought that American quilts were made from scraps of leftover cloth pieced together by thrifty housewives. In fact, there is much evidence within the quilts themselves —for example, in those that employ large panels of previously unused fabrics—to support a theory that many women bought new fabrics for their quilts. Pieced block patterns made it possible to display a great number of the latest brightly colored American cottons.

The diamond-shaped pieces that form the stars on this quilt had to be joined with great precision, since uneven stitching would have prevented the stars from lying flat. The arrangement of the fabric pieces was, of course, also a matter of major concern. At first glance, all the smaller stars appear identical in their color progression: They all start with a red center, as is traditional in Star of Bethlehem quilts, and radiate outward in rings of tan, brown, blue, red, tan, and red. One, however, is different: In the middle star of the bottom border, the red center is surrounded by rings of blue, brown, tan, red, tan, and red. Its color scheme, alone among those of all the small stars, repeats the scheme of the large central star. Was this irregularity intentional, or did the rigors of piec-ing so many diamonds cause the quiltmaker to slip?

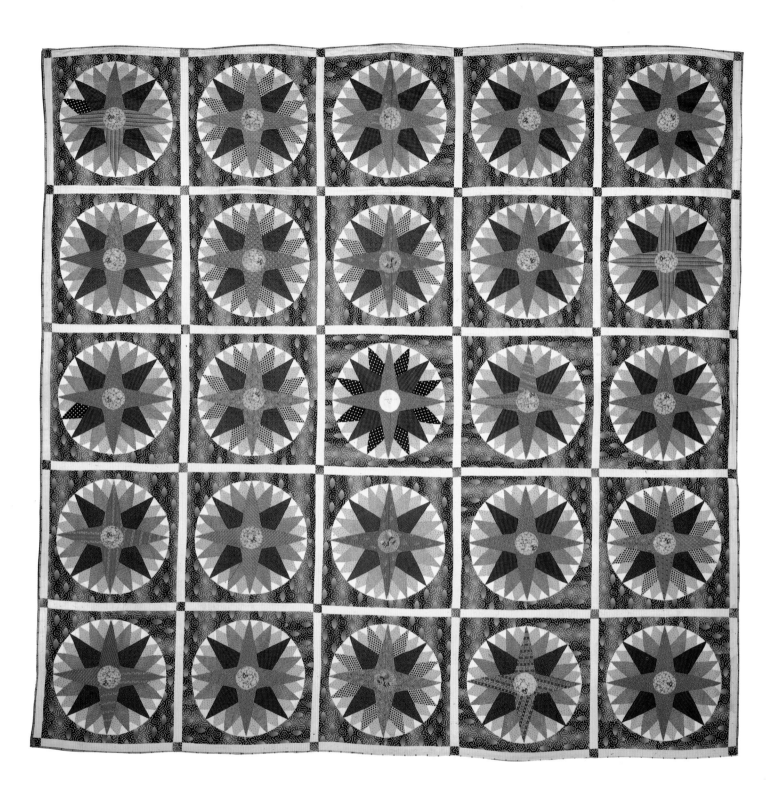

9. Mariner's Compass Quilt

Barbara Ann Miller
Pennsylvania, 1847
Cotton and linen
Promised Gift of The Hascoe Foundation (L1988.55)

This beautiful Pennsylvania Mariner's Compass quilt is signed in ink in the very center: *Barbara Ann Miller/her quilt/1847.* It exemplifies the German approach to the English tradition of quiltmaking rather than the more purely British style that flourished in Pennsylvania at the same time. Several factors contribute to the supposition that Miller was of Pennsylvania-German background. First of all, even today, Miller is one of the most common names found in the Pennsylvania counties with large Germanic populations. Second, the quilt is pieced of strongly colored cottons. Pennsylvania-German quilts are typically more boldly colored and patterned than those from other areas of the Northeast. This emphasis on ornate patterning is thought to reflect the influence of the German and central European folk-art traditions that the Pennsylvania-Germans had carried with them to America. Third, the Mariner's Compass quilt pattern is among the most popular sewn by Pennsylvania-German women. It demands a great deal of care in both cutting and stitching the many small pieces that make up each compass. On this quilt, the compass points are pieced out of a variety of colored cottons, all printed with small-scale patterns, which differ from compass to compass. The only fabrics that do not vary from block to block are the yellow cotton used for the outermost points and the white linen pieces that fill in the circles.

The most striking element of the quilt is the spectacular background fabric of each compass block. This green and burnt-orange rainbow print was very likely printed in England. It is used in such quantity that it must have been bought specifically to make this quilt. First produced in England in the 1820s, by the late 1840s rainbow prints had become extremely intricate and vivid, as the fabric in this quilt testifies. The backing cloth is a blue and white rainbow print that is almost identical to a swatch in an English sample book (156.415/Sa4Q/ No.107290) of about 1840 in the Metropolitan's collection. Another unusual characteristic is the use of plain white linen sashing to join and outline the blocks. During this period, a fancy pattern was usually pieced or appliquéd on white fabric blocks that were then separated by colored sashing. Our Mariner's Compass quilt employs a reversal of that typical scheme to achieve its full effect.

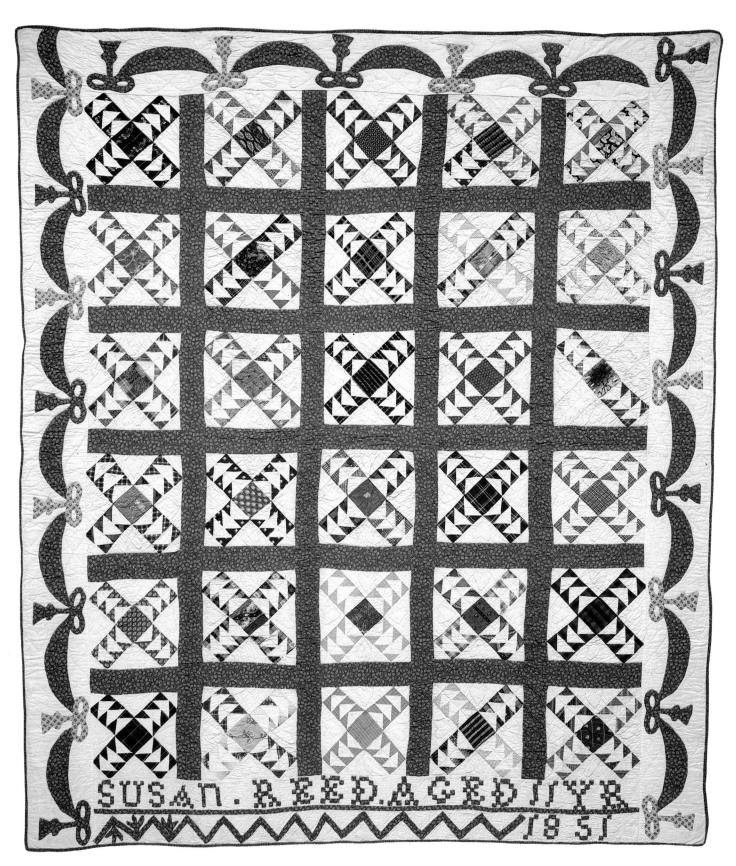

10. Wild Goose Chase Quilt

Susan Reed Ruddick (1839–1869)
Forestburgh, Sullivan County, New York, 1851
Cotton
Gift of Mrs. William Rhinelander Stewart, 1976 (1976.198.1)

11. Log Cabin Crib Quilt

Probably Anna Susan Ruddick Trowbridge (1869–1949)
Monticello, Sullivan County, New York, about 1875
Cotton and wool
Gift of Mrs. William Rhinelander Stewart, 1976 (1976.198.2)

12. Nine Patch Quilt

Anna Susan Ruddick Trowbridge (1869–1949)
Monticello, Sullivan County, New York, 1877
Cotton
Gift of Mrs. William Rhinelander Stewart, 1976 (1976.198.3)

Susan Reed, who made this delightful quilt (catalogue no. 10) in the pattern called Wild Goose Chase, was born and raised in Forestburgh, Sullivan County, New York, where she became a schoolteacher at the Hartwood School. Reed's marriage certificate (Figure 5), family register (Figure 6), some family photos (Figures 7, 8), six letters written to her future husband, and two quilts made by her daughter (catalogue nos. 11, 12) were donated to the Museum along with this quilt.

Susan Reed was born on July 25, 1839, the oldest child of Isaac and Elvina Drake Reed. Her father, who was a farmer and a lumber dealer, held a number of public offices in Forestburgh, including the job of Town Clerk in 1864. That same year, the Town Supervisor was John Ruddick (see Figure 7), owner of a lumber mill, who was to be Reed's husband. John was a widower; he had been married in 1847 to Catherine A. Green, who died in 1862. The earliest of the extant courtship letters from Susan to John is dated February 14, 1866. She was then twenty-six, and he was forty-three. The letter begins:

> My Friend,
>   Having a new pen & being anxious to test its qualities, I don't know as I could do it better than by writing you a *valentine*; for you know or *ought* to know that today is the day sacred to St. Valentine. He must have been an amorous Saint judging by the epistles full of loves & doves flying about on the day called Valentine's day.
>   Did I say I would write you a Valentine? Well I think I will not (for if I did it would be the first I ever wrote) but instead will try to write a

Figure 5. Reed/Ruddick Marriage Certificate. Signed April 2, 1868. Form published by E. Goodenough, New York City, 1866. Etching and engraving, inscriptions in ink, 10 × 14 in. The Metropolitan Museum of Art, Gift of Mrs. William Rhinelander Stewart, 1976 (1976.649.2)

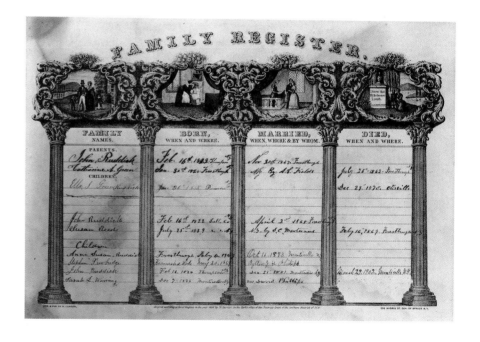

Figure 6. Ruddick Family Register. Begun in 1847. Form published by Nathaniel Currier, New York City, 1846. Colored lithograph, inscriptions in ink, 10¹/₁₆ × 14 in. The Metropolitan Museum of Art, Gift of Mrs. William Rhinelander Stewart, 1976 (1976.649.1)

plain common sense letter if I can collect thoughts enough to do such a thing. Some-times I find it difficult (after teaching all day) to collect material for a letter much less putting it in shape.

After much discussion of the doings of friends and the local Methodist church to which they both belonged, Reed ended her letter: "Now I will close by bidding you good night, assuring you of all the best wishes of one who feels a deep interest in your welfare. I shall expect an answer—Sue."

11

12

The next letter that survives, dated November 12, 1866, shows that Reed was still using her excellent sewing skills. Sewing, however, was not foremost in her mind: "Being alone tonight I set myself sewing for a time, but my thoughts were busyer than my needle, consequently the sewing was discarded altogether, and reading took its place; failing to become interested in my book + a spirit of loneliness creeping over me I thought I would write a bit."

In the next letter, dated December 31, 1866, it becomes obvious that some sort of problem was keeping the pair from making their friendship public:

> My Friend,
>   When I last saw you, you asked me to write you once in a while, which I refused to do, giving as a reason, the existing circumstances which it is not necessary to mention to you; but I thought the matter over and came to the conclusion that under the existing state of things no wrong could possibly accrue from a friendly correspondence between us; hence the letter you will receive. . . .
>   I have already written longer than I intended and will close hoping you will not preserve this scrawl. I need not ask you to answer for had you not intended to do so you would not have asked me to write you. I have written nothing with which the most fastidious could find fault therefore no wrong can come of it, even if this should fall in the hands of one of the gossips of our small town—it would be a mystery to them.
>   Your sincere friend, S. R.

Anger and disappointment are expressed in a letter dated July 22, 1867, which reveals the nature of the problem. John was involved with another woman before he became friendly with Susan, and that "certain lady," as Susan refers to her, has made it widely known that she disapproves of Susan's friendship with a man to whom she has a prior claim. Susan wrote to John:

> Your interview must have been a stormy one judging from the indignant manner in which her private opinion was publicly expressed. I am sorry I am the unfortunate offender. . . . What the result of the interview was I do not know as I took no pains to inquire but I suppose you are on probation again provided you will not be "running after every thing." John, that expression hurt me not a little, as I thought you had kept no company but mine besides hers, for the last eight or nine months, at least I thought you had not. The every thing must mean me. . . . I may have done wrong in receiving attention to which she alone had a right but you know all about it—how it was and the result.

Susan goes on to tell John about a job offer she has received to become head of a junior school in a town some distance from Forestburgh. Perhaps at that moment, the idea of moving away from Forestburgh seemed very compelling. Somehow, the conflict was settled. The last letter in the group, written in November 1867, is a chatty discussion of a visit Susan was making to some friends in another town; it mentions nothing of the circumstances set forth in the previous letter. The couple was married on April 2, 1868. Unfortunately, Reed's story does not end on this happy note. She became pregnant soon after she was married and on February 4, 1869, gave birth to a daughter, Anna Susan Ruddick. Reed died twelve days later at the age of twenty-nine and was buried in the Forestburgh cemetery.

It is believed that Anna Ruddick (see Figure 8) made both the unsigned Log Cabin crib quilt and the signed Nine Patch quilt illustrated here. The crib quilt is awkwardly constructed and seems to be the work of a child. The fabrics used to construct it can be dated to the 1870s, the period when Anna would most likely have sewn it. Although her full-sized quilt is not as beautifully made as her mother's (it must be kept in mind she was only *eight* years old), it is obvious that Anna looked to Susan's quilt for inspiration. After Susan Reed's death, her mother, Elvina Reed, moved to Monticello, New York, where John was living, to take care of baby Anna. She remained there until John remarried in 1881. Since it was probably Elvina Reed who directed both Susan and Anna in the making of their quilts, it is not surprising that the two quilts are similar. Both are constructed of blocks with a border on three sides. The fourth edge of each quilt is signed and dated in letters made up of small appliquéd squares that simulate pieced work. The large scale of the signatures is unusual; it is more common to see an inscription of this size on the embroidered blankets and whitework coverlets of the early nineteenth century. Elvina probably learned to sew during that period and passed on the style of the earlier era to her daughter and granddaughter.

Although we have Anna Susan Ruddick's photograph, we know little about her life. She was married at the age of twenty-four to Stephen Trowbridge, the owner of a very successful lumber business that still exists in Monticello. They had three children: Ruddick Trowbridge, who was a machine gunner in World War I and was killed in action in France in 1918, Sherwood "Hop" Trowbridge, and Louise Trowbridge Hamilton. Louise had no children to inherit the family quilts; they were sold in an estate sale that took place after her death, and their purchaser eventually donated them to the Museum.

Figure 7. Photograph of John Ruddick
(1822–1902), about 1885. The Metropolitan
Museum of Art, Gift of Mrs. William Rhinelander
Stewart, 1976

Figure 8. Photograph of Anna Ruddick Trowbridge, about
1895. The Metropolitan Museum of Art, Gift of Mrs. William
Rhinelander Stewart, 1976

13. Double X Quilt

Maker unknown
Probably Lancaster, Fairfield County, Ohio, 1849
Cotton
Gift of Mrs. Emanuel Altman, 1962 (62.145)

Soon after her marriage in the early 1890s, Rachel Moskovits moved from Cleveland to Lancaster, Ohio, a smaller city in the center of the state. According to her niece, the donor of this quilt, Mrs. Moskovits received it during the early days of her marriage as a gift from the wife of a local farmer. The family always supposed that it was given to her because her name matched the initials *R M* that appear on the quilt.

This is a simple quilt, but in its simplicity, it is an object of great beauty. The front and backing are of plain white cotton, and the diamond-set blocks and narrow zigzag borders are pieced with a dark blue cotton printed with a tiny white dot. The quilting is very fine, with a particularly beautiful feather vine border that terminates at each of the corners in a feather wreath. In the lower right corner (see detail below), the feather wreath contains the quilted inscription: *R M/1849.*

When viewed alongside other quilts in our collection, this work relates most closely to our Pinwheel and silk Crazy quilts (catalogue nos. 30, 31). Interestingly, each of these two quilts originated in a group that set itself apart from the mainstream of American life: The first was made by an Amish quiltmaker in Indiana in 1930, and the second was probably made by a Quaker woman during the 1880s. It seems that both quiltmakers were following the simple midwestern model illustrated by this piece, in which a field of diamond-shaped blocks is set within a wide, intricately quilted border.

Detail of catalogue no. 13

14. Oak Leaf Quilt

Maker unknown
Possibly Rhinebeck, Dutchess County, New York, about 1860
Cotton
Purchase, Mrs. Roger Brunschwig Gift, 1988 (1988.24.2)

In this quilt, simple materials have been used to create a striking effect. Dark blue printed cotton is appliquéd on a white ground in twelve blocks, each containing an organic motif traditionally known as an Oak Leaf. The border figures, edge binding, and sashing are cut from the same blue fabric. Because of the sprightly hearts that flank the flowers along the border, it is tempting to call this a bride's quilt. Its excellent condition and overall quality suggest that if it was not intended to be a bridal quilt, it is certainly a best quilt, one of a type used primarily to display the skills of its maker.

The quilt was found in Rhinebeck, Dutchess County, New York, and shares certain characteristics with other mid-nineteenth-century quilts made in southeastern New York State. Rounded, abstracted figures such as the oak leaves seen here are found on many of these quilts. The shapes of the oak leaves and of the plants, hearts, and flowers that make up the border were most likely achieved by using cut-paper templates. These templates were made by folding a square or circle of paper in half, or in the case of the eight-petaled flowers, in quarters, and cutting out a design, in much the same way that children make cut-paper snowflakes. This technique is most commonly associated with the appliquéd quilts of Hawaii, but it also seems to have been popular in the southeastern part of New York State. Our Album quilt from Fishkill in Dutchess County (catalogue no. 18) has many blocks decorated with cut-paper designs, and the maker of our Pineapple quilt (p. 211) from Glen Head in Nassau County used this technique to form the appliquéd designs.

15. Eagle Quilt

Maker unknown
Possibly New England, about 1837–50
Cotton
Gift of Mrs. Jacob M. Kaplan, 1974 (1974.32)

After the Great Seal of the United States was adopted by the Continental Congress in 1782, the image of the American eagle became an extremely popular design element, used to adorn all types of late eighteenth- and early nineteenth-century decorative art objects. The eagle motif was employed with great sophistication by the cabinetmakers of Federal America; however, its appearance on handmade quilts is often whimsical.

Although many Eagle quilts were made at the time of the nation's Centennial in 1876, the Museum's Eagle quilt, which unfortunately came to us with no provenance, is thought to have been made a few decades earlier. Centennial-era quilts often feature four eagles, one in each corner, their wings outspread and their heads all facing center instead of the large single eagle at the center of this quilt. In addition, the twenty-six stars above the eagle's head may provide a significant clue to the date of our quilt. In 1837, Michigan was admitted to the Union as the twenty-sixth state, and since national events were often commemorated by quiltmakers, this piece may well have been made in celebration of that event. Lastly, the printed cottons pieced and appliquéd into the quilt appear to date from the 1830s and 1840s. The blue and white stripe in the zigzag border is particularly distinctive; it could be an American attempt to emulate the English rainbow prints so popular during those years.

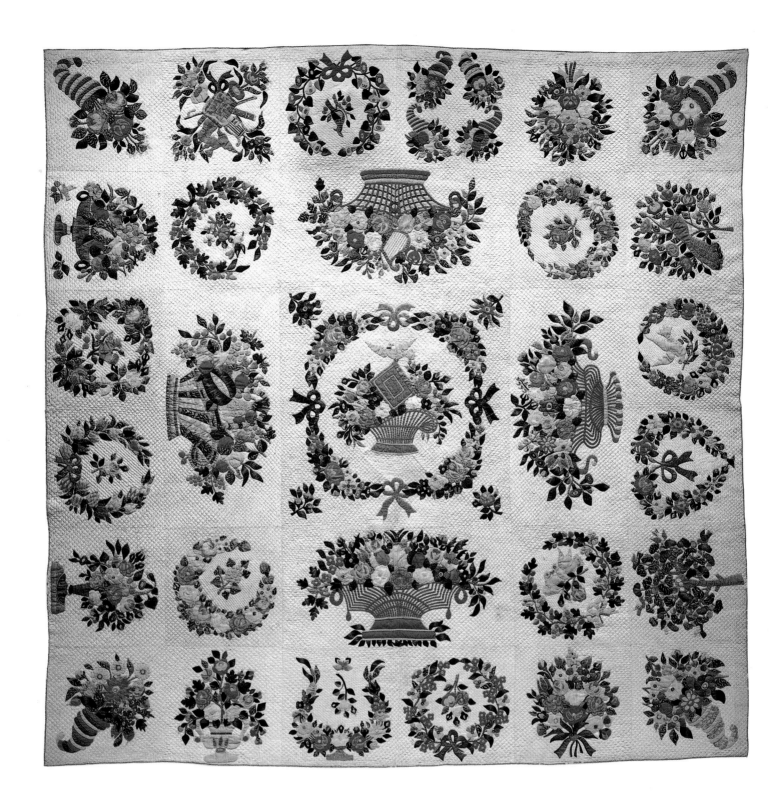

16. Presentation Quilt

Probably Mary Evans (1829–1916)
Baltimore, Maryland, about 1849
Cotton and silk velvet
Sansbury-Mills Fund, 1974 (1974.24)

An extraordinary tour de force, this Baltimore Presentation quilt is decorated with vibrant floral wreaths, delicate baskets of fruits and flowers, and assorted birds, all superbly appliquéd onto the plain white backing with multicolored cottons. It is most likely the work of Mary Evans (1829–1916), who is thought to have worked as a professional quiltmaker during the 1840s and 1850s. It is one of over a dozen quilts and numerous quilt blocks that have been attributed to her on the basis of similarities in motifs, in sewing and appliquéing techniques, and in the handwriting on the inscriptions. Unfortunately, since there is no known work signed by Mary Evans, no quilt can be absolutely confirmed as hers.

Mary Evans, the daughter of a bricklayer, lived with her family in a small house on the corner of Gough and Eden streets in Baltimore. She was seventeen when her father died, leaving her mother with ten children to support. Mary Evans was a member of the Methodist Church. According to a theory proposed by Dena Katzenberg, an expert on Baltimore quilts, it is through that association that she met a woman named Achsah Goodwin Wilkins (1775–1854). Mrs. Wilkins seems to have taught a number of poor young Methodist women how to sew and design quilts, among them Mary Evans (and Elizabeth Morrison; see catalogue no. 17). Mrs. Wilkins was the daughter of a wealthy Baltimore merchant, and her husband and father-in-law jointly owned a dry goods store. It can therefore be assumed that she had access to the quantities of fancy printed cottons that were coming into the active mid-nineteenth-century port of Baltimore from England and France. It is known that she designed intricate coverlets appliquéd with colorful chintzes, which have been passed down through the generations of her family. According to family tradition, because Mrs. Wilkins had a skin disease that prevented her from doing her own sewing, she designed and laid out coverlets and then had them stitched by others. Katzenberg hypothesizes that Mrs. Wilkins, acting as a patron, took young Methodist women such as Mary Evans under her wing. She supplied these quiltmakers with money or fine fabrics and with the use of her home, where they sewed quilts based on the older chintz models. But whereas the earlier quilts were made with flat single-layer chintz appliqués, these young women built up the floral wreath and basket motifs characteristic of chintz designs out of small separate bits of brightly colored fabric, both solid and printed. Although this type of quilt, in which each square is decorated with a different motif, is commonly called an Album quilt, a true Album quilt is made up of blocks that have been contributed by numerous different makers. (For examples of Album quilts, see catalogue nos. 17, 18.) Since the quilt illustrated here was made by only one person, most likely to commemorate a specific occasion, it is better described as a Presentation quilt.

The Museum's quilt is something of a puzzle. Another quilt attributed to Mary Evans, now in the collection of the Baltimore Museum of Art, was commissioned by the parents of Elizabeth Sliver and, after its completion, presented to Elizabeth as a wedding gift. Because it is extremely similar to our quilt and is inscribed *1849*, the same date has been assigned to our work. Underneath that quilt's central basket, which is nearly identical to the one on the Metropolitan's quilt, there is an inscription to Elizabeth Sliver from her parents. Our quilt once had such an inscription as well, but it was cut away before the piece was quilted, and a plain white patch of fabric was inserted in its place. Did another young woman, for whom this quilt was intended, suddenly break off her wedding plans? Was the quilt then sold to another client, or did the original client purchase the piece anyway, without any inscription to mark some special event? Since it came into the Museum's collection without a provenance, we may never know the true history of our beautiful Baltimore quilt.

Detail of catalogue no. 16

17. Album Quilt

Members of the Brown and Turner families
Baltimore, Maryland, begun in 1846
Cotton
Bequest of Margaret Brown Potvin, 1987 (1988.134)

The Museum was given this lively Baltimore quilt in 1988. It is a true Album quilt, since almost every block is signed and dated by a different person, unlike our other, more sophisticated Baltimore quilt (catalogue no. 16), which is thought to be the work of a single maker. Most of this Album quilt's blocks were appliquéd by members of the Brown and Turner families. Some of the blocks are decorated with motifs that are typically found only on Baltimore quilts, such as the central eagle and flag, while other designs, such as those that employ the cut-paper technique, can be seen on Album quilts from all regions of the country.

A bequest from Margaret Brown Davis Potvin (1897–1987), the quilt entered our collection with almost no known history. The only information came from the donor, who mentioned to the executor of her will that her grandmother Margaret Brown Turner Schenck made the quilt. After much research, we were able to ascertain why it was made and to identify almost all of the people who contributed blocks (Figure 9).

When we received this work, we did not know Schenck's birth and death dates, but by counting back two generational spans of about twenty-five years each, we reached the conclusion that she must have been born around 1850. Because most of the blocks were dated between 1846 and 1852, she would have been too young to be the quilt's maker, and it was therefore surmised that Mrs. Potvin's great-grandmother must have made the quilt. Having noted the Brown family's tradition of naming their girls Margaret (Mrs. Potvin's mother was also named Margaret), we assumed that the Margaret L. Brown who signed the quilt (block 1B) must have been Mrs. Potvin's great-grandmother. The only man's name on the quilt was Francis Turner (1816–1858; block 3B), and since we knew that Mrs. Potvin's grandmother's last name was Turner, we assumed that Margaret L. Brown married Francis Turner around the time the quilt was made and that the quilt blocks were given to her as engagement presents.

Two facts shattered this theory. First, a closer examination of the quilt revealed that the blocks were attached to the sashing by machine stitching. Although invented in the 1840s, sewing machines were not widely available before the 1860s. Therefore, it did seem more likely that Mrs. Potvin's grandmother Margaret Brown Turner Schenck had actually made the quilt (i.e., joined the blocks and quilted the layers together). Further genealogical research revealed that Francis Turner had married Mary Brown (1818–1871), not Margaret L. Brown, on November 14, 1839. Mary Brown Turner (block 2E) was Margaret Potvin's great-grandmother. The birth date of Margaret Brown Turner Schenck was subsequently found to be July 31, 1847, and we now theorize that the quilt blocks were given to Mary Brown Turner by her friends and family in celebration of the coming birth of her child. For some reason, she never joined the blocks together, and the daughter in whose honor the blocks were made completed the quilt perhaps twenty years later.

Because the blocks are signed in many different types of handwriting, it can be assumed that most were actually made by those who signed them. We have already identified Mary Brown Turner as the recipient of the quilt and the block made for her husband. Similarities in fabrics and stitching techniques cause us to believe that Francis's block 3B was most likely made by his mother, Susanna Mumma Turner (about 1787–1854), who also contributed block 5E and probably made unmarked block 2C as well. Block 4C, which shares many fabrics with Susanna's blocks, is signed by Mary Brown Turner's mother, Jane Lockard Brown (1791–1867).

Mary Brown Turner's sisters also contributed to the quilt. They were Margaret L. Brown (about 1822–1849; block 1B), Helen Brown (block 2D), and Jane L. Brown Creamer (1820–?; block 2B). Susan Amanda Turner (block 5B) was Francis Turner's sister.

There are four very similar blocks on the quilt that are decorated with wreaths. Three are dated March 18, 1847, and one is dated March 9, 1847. Mary Brown Turner's block 2E is one of these, as is her sister Margaret's block 1B. The other two blocks of this type, 4B and 5D, are signed with the names of Mary's two young daughters, Susan I. Turner (about 1842–?) and Mary E. Turner (about 1845–?). Margaret L. Brown's block shares fabric and fine sewing technique, as well as the same handwriting on the inscription, with the blocks signed Susan I. and Mary E. Turner, and we assume therefore that she made these two blocks for her sister's quilt.

Blocks 1A and 3C, which are much more intricately appliquéd than the others, were made by Elizabeth Morrison and Mary Ann O'Laughlen, respectively. The names of both these women also appear on other Baltimore Album quilts. Elizabeth Morrison has been identified as a member of the same Methodist Church as Achsah Goodwin Wilkins, who was probably the teacher of a number of professional and semiprofessional quilters. A spectacular quilt now in the collection of the Saint Louis Art Museum was presented to Elizabeth Morrison by her quilting group, called the "Ladies of Baltimore." Blocks signed by Elizabeth Morrison found in other quilts are of uniformly high quality, close to the standard of the work assumed to be by the famous Mary Evans. This is also true of blocks signed by Mary Ann O'Laughlen, the stepdaughter of Samuel Williams, a lay preacher connected with the Exeter Street Methodist Church, the church attended by the Browns and the Turners. O'Laughlen's name appears along with the names of members of the Brown and Turner families on a quilt now in the collection of the Baltimore Museum of Art, which was made for her stepfather. Although not as delicate, her blocks are made in the same style as those commonly attributed to Mary Evans. One must surmise, therefore, that there may have been a number of professional/semiprofessional makers of Baltimore Album quilts, and that it is a mistake to automatically assign the name Mary Evans to every high-quality quilt of this type.

	A	B	C	D	E
1	Elizabeth Morrison	Margaret L. Brown March 18th 1847	Ann Brown Baltimore January 29th 1847	Rachel D. Taylor May 1847	M. A. Hook [cross-stitched]
2	Elizabeth D. Dobler 1847	Jane L. Creamer Baltimore Dec. 15, 1846	unmarked	Helen Brown Baltimore January 29th 1846	Mary Turner March 18th 1847
3	unmarked	Francis Turner March 2 1847	Mary Ann O'Laughlen/ 1846	Mary A. Dobler	M A H 1852 [cross-stitched]
4	Frances Leivis	Susan I. Turner Baltimore March 18th 1847	Jane Brown March 6th 1847	Agnes A. S. House March 8th 1847	unmarked
5	Mary E. Doretee March 9th 1847	Susan Amanda Turner	May 13/ Presented by M.W. Conal/ 1846 [cross-stitched]	Mary E. Turner March 9th 1847	Susanna Turner March 1st 1847

Figure 9. Diagram of Album quilt (catalogue no. 17), showing inscriptions. All signatures in ink, each by a different hand, except where otherwise indicated.

18. Album Quilt

Members of the First Reformed Churches of Fishkill and Hopewell,
Dutchess County, New York, about 1855–60
Cotton
Gift of Miss Eliza Polhemus Cobb, 1952 (52.103)

This boldly graphic Album quilt, in the shades of green and red most favored by mid-nineteenth-century quiltmakers, is one of the most visually delightful quilts in our collection. Album, or Signature quilts, as they were sometimes called, were extremely popular in the middle of the nineteenth century and were made in every part of the country. They often commemorated a particular event (see, for example, catalogue no. 17), such as a birth, marriage, retirement, or leave-taking. Sometimes, however, this type of quilt was made purely to acknowledge and give expression to the bonds of friendship that linked those who contributed to them.

Although the signatures of individual makers do appear on some of its blocks (Figure 10), neither dates nor place names appear on this quilt. Without that information, it was difficult to determine where the piece, which has been in the Museum's collection for more than thirty-five years, was made. Recently, however, a scholar recognized that a number of the names signed are those of Dutch families who settled in the southeastern portion of New York State. An examination of the New York State Census of 1850 revealed that all the somewhat unusual last names signed on our quilt could be found in Dutchess County, New York, and, even more specifically, clustered around the town of Fishkill. The records of the Dutch First Reformed churches for Fishkill and neighboring Hopewell reinforced the conclusion that this work was made in Dutchess County. Two of the signers are actually named in the records: Susan Adriana Monfort (block 2E) was born on December 11, 1811, to Stephen Monfort and Aletta Adriance Monfort and was baptized at the church in Hopewell, and Harriet E. Monfort (block 4B) gave birth to many children, the first in 1828, who were baptized at the same church. The family names of all the other signers turned up time and time again in church records. And gravestone inscriptions in the Fishkill cemetery show that members of the Van Wyck (block 5E) and Rapalje (block 3C) families often married each other.

On the basis of purely stylistic criteria, the quilt could be dated anywhere between 1840 and 1870. Nevertheless, a date of about 1855–60 at the earliest seems most likely, because although the rest of it is hand stitched, the white cotton edge binding has been sewn to the quilt by machine. A sewing machine would probably have been unavailable to the makers before about 1860. The binding could have been added at a later date, but judging from the way the fabrics have aged, it appears to have been stitched at the same time as the rest of the quilt.

For a utilitarian job such as attaching binding, the sewing machine was considered the answer to a prayer. In November 1860, about the time this quilt was made, *Godey's Lady's Book* (p. 463) extolled the virtues of the new machine:

> *The Sewing Machine* should be here named as the completement of the art of needlework. It, the *machine,* will do all the drudgeries of sewing, thus leaving time for the perfecting of the beautiful in woman's handiwork. We have dealt often on this wonderful invention, and wish it were possible to interest all our readers in this new romance of needlework, where aid more potent than any ever suggested by fairydom and all elfs of fancy, is so easily obtained that we wonder any woman who has a family to make clothing for can do without a *sewing machine.* A writer in the *New York Observer* says of the Wheeler and Wilson sewing machine; "It is the one we use, and an institution we shall never dispense with so long as the Union endures."
>
> The Union may be dissolved, but the sewing machine will be used as long as civilization continues.

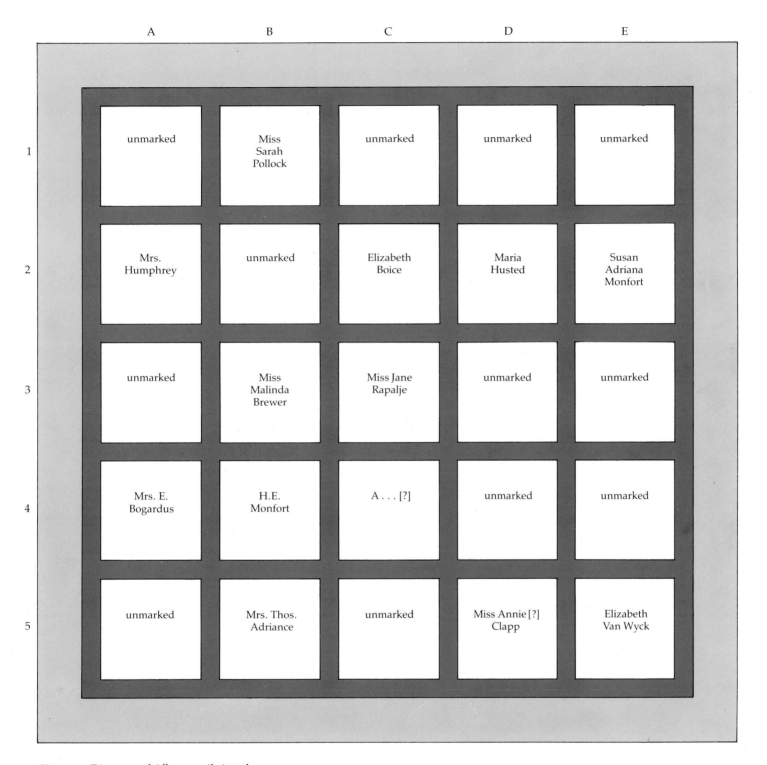

	A	B	C	D	E
1	unmarked	Miss Sarah Pollock	unmarked	unmarked	unmarked
2	Mrs. Humphrey	unmarked	Elizabeth Boice	Maria Husted	Susan Adriana Monfort
3	unmarked	Miss Malinda Brewer	Miss Jane Rapalje	unmarked	unmarked
4	Mrs. E. Bogardus	H.E. Monfort	A . . . [?]	unmarked	unmarked
5	unmarked	Mrs. Thos. Adriance	unmarked	Miss Annie [?] Clapp	Elizabeth Van Wyck

Figure 10. Diagram of Album quilt (catalogue no. 18), showing inscriptions. All signatures in ink, each by a different hand.

19. Log Cabin Quilt (Straight Furrow variation)

Maker unknown
United States, about 1865
Wool and cotton
Purchase, Eva Gebhard-Gourgaud Foundation Gift and funds from
various donors, 1974 (1974.37)

20. Log Cabin Quilt (Light and Dark variation)

Maker unknown
Possibly Pennsylvania, about 1865
Wool and cotton
Purchase, Eva Gebhard-Gourgaud Foundation Gift, 1973
(1973.159)

The two quilts shown here, pieced mainly of printed wool challises, are good examples of the American Log Cabin style first popular around the middle of the nineteenth century. A Log Cabin quilt is always made in square units or blocks, each with one diagonal half of dark strips and the other of light strips. These blocks can be set together in different ways to form any of a variety of overall patterns. (One exception is the Pineapple variation of the Log Cabin pattern; see catalogue no. 28.) In the Straight Furrow variation (catalogue no. 19), a pattern is created by alternating the direction of the square blocks as they are joined across the width of the quilt. In the Light and Dark variation (catalogue no. 20), the squares are placed to create a pattern of light and dark diamond shapes. The technique of stitching a Log Cabin quilt differs from that employed for most pieced quilts (except for Crazy quilts) in that the small strips of fabric are anchored to a square of foundation fabric. Although both the Museum's bed covers are quilted around the edges of each small strip of fabric, it is not unusual for Log Cabin quilts to be unquilted. The quilt top is made up of what amounts to a double layer of wool strips in addition to the foundation layer and thus is heavier than most pieced tops. Therefore, Log Cabin quilts are commonly finished without batting between the layers and with decorative threads at intervals tying the front to the backing.

Although Log Cabin quilts have for many years been cited as the most American of all quilts, that judgment has recently undergone some revision. The traditional view was supported by Caulfeild and Saward's 1882 *Dictionary of*

19

20

Needlework, a British publication that referred to a patchwork similar to Log Cabin piecing but made up of small pieces of silk ribbons, as "American or Canadian Patchwork." Although the two are constructed in the same manner, the effect achieved with the silk ribbons is quite different from that of the wool Log Cabin quilts most commonly found in America, and in fact, "American or Canadian Patchwork" ribbon quilts are far rarer today than wool or cotton Log Cabin quilts.

Early examples of Log Cabin piecing that exist in Great Britain are cited in two well-known books about British quilts. In her book *Patchwork* (p. 66), Averil Colby describes a Log Cabin quilt of tweed and homespun wool made from a pattern that had been handed down through a single Scottish family since 1745. In *Quilts of the British Isles* (p. 68), Janet Rae discusses a number of possible origins for the pattern. For American works, it is commonly accepted that the strips of fabric represent the logs of an American cabin and the traditional red center square signifies the hearth. However, the most fascinating of Rae's theories holds that the pattern actually reproduces the appearance of strip-farmed land in the countryside of seventeenth-century Scotland. Extending this interpretation logically, she concludes that the red center square represents the sun shining on the fields rather than the glowing hearth of an American pioneer's home. According to this hypothesis, the Log Cabin quilt originated in Great Britain hundreds of years ago and was adopted by nineteenth-century Americans after it journeyed across the ocean.

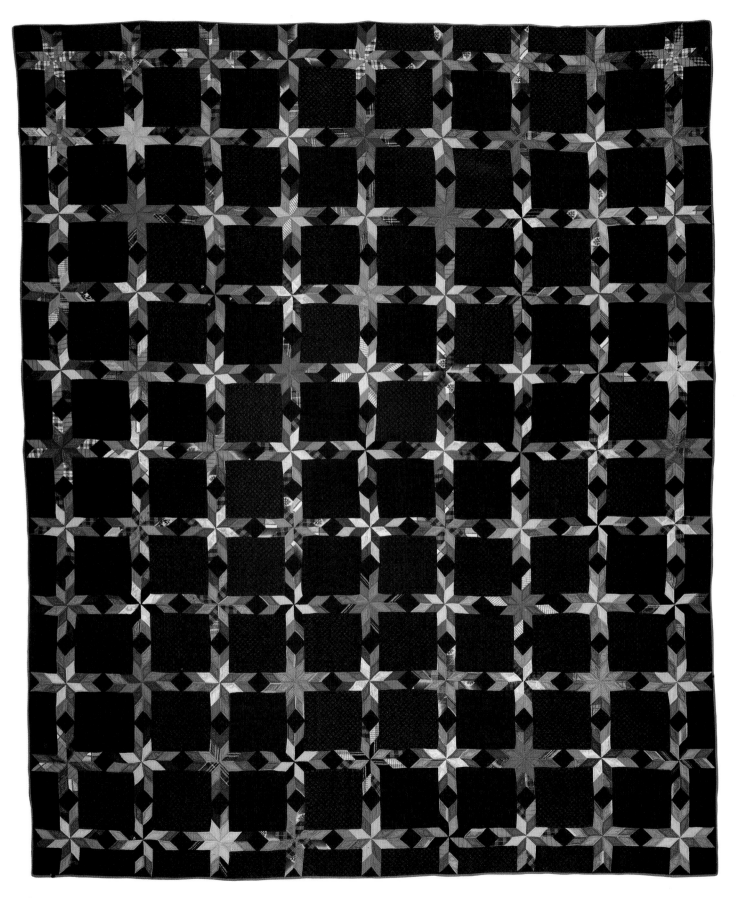

21

21. Touching Star of Lemoyne Quilt

Maker unknown
United States, about 1860
Silk and cotton
Gift of Mrs. Gilbert Chapman, 1974 (1974.154)

22. Fruit Baskets Quilt

Maker unknown
Possibly Providence, Rhode Island, about 1860
Silk and silk velvet
Gift of Mr. and Mrs. Samuel Schwartz, 1975 (1975.95)

23. Broken Dishes Quilt

Maker unknown
Possibly Ohio, about 1920
Silk and cotton
Sansbury-Mills Fund, 1973 (1973.205)

Amongst the most amusing labors of the needle, that of patchwork
will, by many be accepted as the first. It offers great variety in its
progress, producing many striking effects by means of exercising taste
in all its combinations. In fact, this *parqueterie* of the work-table
requires more of the qualities of the artist than might once have been
imagined. It demands a knowledge of the power of form and the value
of color. Patchwork is not now what it was a few centuries ago.

When this commentary was published in *Godey's Lady's Book* in February
1860 (p. 163), silk quilts similar to the ones illustrated here were becoming increasingly popular. Silk quilts were made primarily for decorative purposes
and were probably brought out only for show, since in comparison to cotton
quilts, they were fragile and difficult to clean. These showpieces often epito-
mize the kind of artistic quality celebrated by *Godey's*.

The silk quilts illustrated here are unusual in both pattern and color scheme.
The makers of these quilts quite clearly relied upon "a knowledge of the power
of form and the value of color." In the first two works, an overall grid of colorful
silk pieces is played off against a somber background. The black ground in our
Touching Star of Lemoyne quilt (catalogue no. 21) may signify that it was a
mourning quilt, since black is an unusual color choice for a bed cover. However,
nothing is known about the quilt's provenance. The small, brilliantly colored
touching stars that form the grid can be considered a pattern variation of the
traditional Star of Lemoyne. Our Fruit Baskets quilt (catalogue no. 22) is said to
have been made in Providence, Rhode Island. Its gray background is charmingly ornamented with meticulously quilted baskets and epergnes, topped by
brightly colored appliquéd velvet fruits and flowers. Stitched to each corner of

the white silk backing is an appliquéd block like the ones on the front. Such intricacies indicate that this quilt was surely made for display.

Silk quilts have a long tradition in America. Made in Massachusetts in about 1704, the Saltonstall quilt (private collection), which is composed of small triangles of silk, is believed to be the earliest known American pieced quilt. (For an illustration, see Patsy and Myron Orlofsky's *Quilts in America*, plate 1.) Quilted silk petticoats (see Figure 11, p. 90) were worn in the eighteenth century by fashion-conscious American women, and whole-cloth silk quilts very similar to those petticoats may be found in a number of collections.

The Quakers of Pennsylvania traditionally made silk quilts throughout the eighteenth and into the nineteenth century. For most Americans, however, it was during the 1850s and 1860s that silk attracted new interest as a favored material for pieced quilts. Dress silks were generally used; these silks were often "weighted," an industrial process in which the cloth was treated with mineral salts to give it more body. Fashions in clothing had changed by mid-century, and fine cotton dresses were being replaced by silks. One reason for this was that silk became more plentiful and less expensive after 1826, when the British government rescinded its prohibition against the importation of French silks. The English silk industry was forced to expand rapidly in order to compete with the better-equipped French manufacturers. Probably borrowing from the technical advances made by their European neighbors, the Americans began to experiment with large-scale silk production during the 1840s. The 1845 edition of Webster's *Encyclopedia of Domestic Economy* (p. 968) notes: "From some specimens of American silk lately sent over to this country [England] there appears to be some reason for supposing that, before long, the material may be produced to a considerable extent in that country." It seems that with more silk being imported from England and France and silk also being produced in this country, Americans had easy access to silks of all types by about 1860.

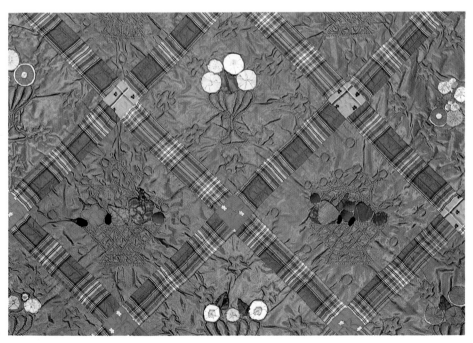

Detail of catalogue no. 22

22

23

Although they were less in vogue than in the latter part of the nineteenth century, silk quilts continued to be made well into the twentieth century. A number of factors indicate that our Broken Dishes quilt (catalogue no. 23) is from the first decades of the twentieth century rather than the last decades of the nineteenth. Its patterning is considerably more random than that of the other two silk quilts in this entry. The somewhat rigid quality of nineteenth-century quilts has been replaced by a quilt top on which the pattern appears to have grown organically; it is hard to decide whether the pieces were first joined in separate blocks or in horizontal, vertical, or even diagonal strips. One opinion suggests that it was pieced from the center outward, which may account for the fact that sections of somewhat incongruous printed fabrics appear only at the outer edges of the quilt. These printed fabrics may not enhance the quilt's overall appearance, but they do help in assigning a date to it, since they are easily identifiable as 1920s-style dress silks. Another clue to this work's approximate age is that the prevalent colors are not those most often associated with the second half of the nineteenth century. Bright yellows, pinks, and oranges like these are more likely to be the colors of the Jazz Age.

24. Mosaic Quilt

Anne Record
New Bedford, Bristol County, Massachusetts, begun in 1864
Silk and silk velvet
Gift of Mrs. Frederick H. Buzzee, 1947 (47.39)

The donor of this silk quilt, Mrs. Frederick H. Buzzee, wrote in a letter to the Museum that it "was begun the day I was born, November 18, 1864, by Miss Anne Record of New Bedford, Massachusetts, a family friend, and designated for me. It took some years in the making, and then was given to me. . . . It has never been used, always carefully preserved, and is in perfect condition." Our quilt was probably made essentially to display Anne Record's artistic skills with the needle. Although at first glance, the arrangement of colors appears random, on closer inspection, subtle diagonal bands of dark and light become apparent. Each rosette is surrounded by six black hexagons, which set the multicolored silks into sharper relief. It is unusual that the back of the quilt (see illustration, p. 74) is also of pieced silk, in this case in a pattern of large squares and rectangles.

The template method of patchwork, which most often employs a hexagon-shaped unit, was introduced into the United States from England both through actual examples and by way of women's periodicals. In 1835, the first patchwork pattern ever published in *Godey's Lady's Book* was for hexagon patchwork, and in the 1850 and 1851 issues, *Godey's* reprinted thirty-five template patterns that had originally appeared in an English magazine called *The Family Friend*. Hexagon patchwork, although never as widely used in the United States as it was in Great Britain, has been popular here from the 1830s to the present. Throughout the nineteenth and into the twentieth century, the basic design scheme of small joined hexagons has remained the same, but the choice of fabrics, the overall patterns in which the hexagons are arranged, the sewing techniques, and the names given this type of quilt have changed.

The earliest hexagon examples, known at the time as Honeycomb quilts, were pieced out of cotton, often in a design with the focus at the center. (An example from our collection is catalogue no. 3.) Frequently, the individual hexagons were stitched together using the overhand or whipstitch. Hexagon bed covers made in the third quarter of the nineteenth century were called Mosaic quilts. They were likely to be pieced out of brilliantly colored silks, as is our quilt. A number of overall patterns were popular. Usually, the hexagons were joined together with the running stitch rather than the more time-consuming whipstitch. Women's magazines of the period recommended displaying Mosaic patchwork in rooms decorated in the Moorish and Turkish styles that were fashionable during the 1870s and 1880s. The name "Mosaic" may also refer to the similarity in appearance of this type of quilt to the colorful tile floors that increasingly decorated many Victorian houses after the invention of encaustic

Back of catalogue no. 24

tiles in the 1830s. Variations on the basic hexagon piece, such as lozenge and octagon shapes, were especially favored in England and were given names like "Pavement Patchwork." One pattern was even named "Minton" after the acclaimed tile factory. The last major revival of the hexagon quilt took place during the 1920s and 1930s. Called Grandmother's Flower Garden quilts, these pastel-colored cotton bed covers were appealing during the Depression years because when pieced completely of scrap fabric, they were inexpensive to make and were thought to look appropriate with the Colonial-Revival-style furniture popular during that period.

Detail of catalogue no. 24

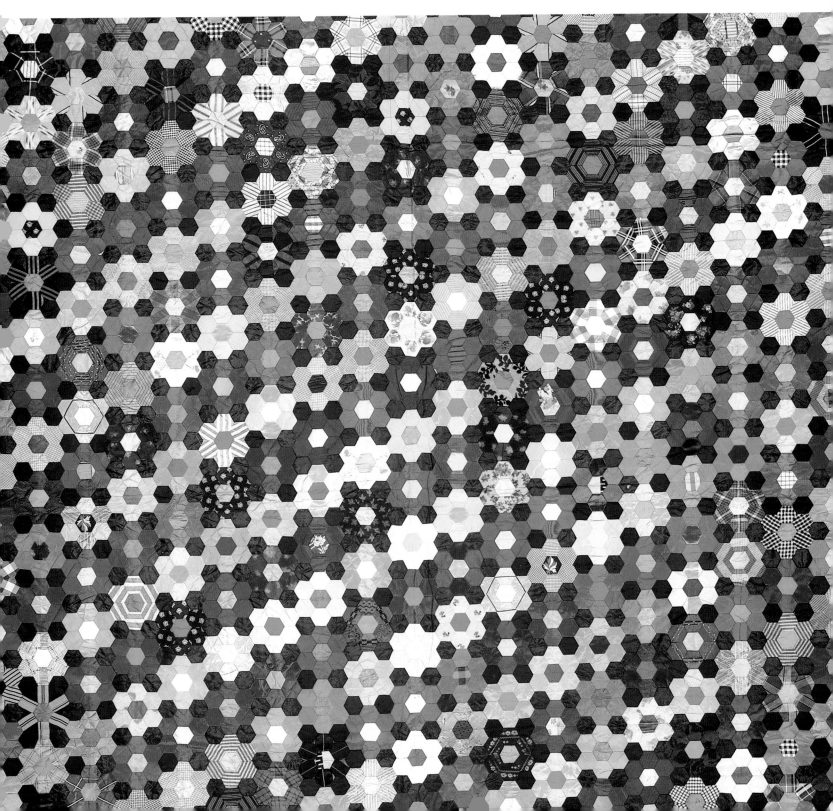

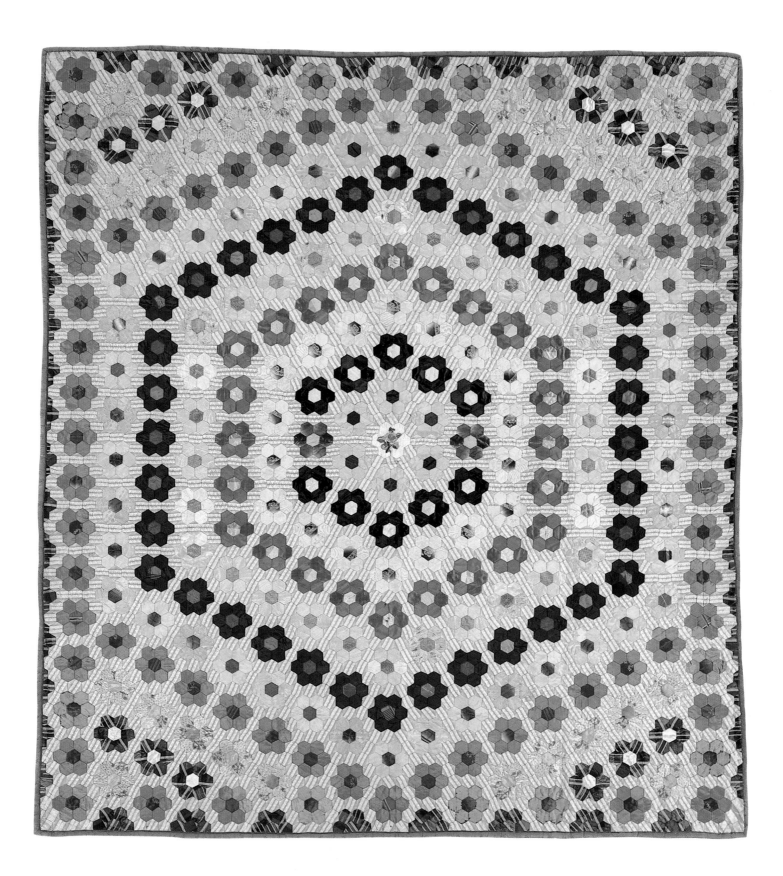

25. Mosaic Quilt

Possibly Caroline Brooks Gould
United States, about 1870
Silk
Bequest of Carolyn Fiske MacGregor, in memory of her
grandmother, Caroline Brooks Gould, 1952 (53.58.1)

Always in search of novel ways to create quilts, women's periodicals of the 1860s encouraged quiltmakers to collect both antique fabrics of historical significance and the signatures of famous people on cloth to include in what were called Autograph quilts. According to Carolyn Fiske MacGregor, the donor of this work, the centermost group of hexagons was pieced from a scrap of George Washington's waistcoat, given by the first president to the donor's great-grandmother, a Mrs. Brooks. The quilt was donated in memory of Mrs. MacGregor's grandmother Caroline Brooks Gould, who may have been its maker. There is a single pink rose embroidered on the center group of hexagons, perhaps as a token of respect to George Washington's memory.

The idea of the Autograph quilt, however, was often taken to further extremes during this period. The best known of this type, the Adeline Harris Sears quilt, has survived. (For an illustration, see Patsy and Myron Orlofsky's *Quilts in America*, plate 60.) That work was discussed extensively in the April 1864 issue of *Godey's Lady's Book*:

> We have lately received a pleasant letter from a young lady of Rhode Island, who is forming a various and valuable collection of Autographs in an original and very womanly way; the design is to insert the names in a counterpane or bed quilt.
>
> Each autograph is written with common black ink, on a diamond shaped piece of white silk, . . . each piece [is] the center of a group of colored diamonds formed in many instances from "storied" fragments of dresses which were worn in the olden days of our country. For instance, there are pieces of a pink satin dress which flaunted at one of President Washington's dinner parties.

After describing at length the number of pieces to go into the quilt and all the famous people (including Washington Irving and six American presidents) who had signed the silk diamonds, *Godey's* concluded:

> In short, we think this autograph bed quilt may be called a very wonderful invention in the way of needlework. . . . Who knows but that in future ages her [Miss Sears's] work may be looked at like the Bayeux Tapestry, not only as a marvel of woman's ingenious and intellectual industry, but as affording an idea of the civilization of our times and also giving a notion of the persons as estimated in history.

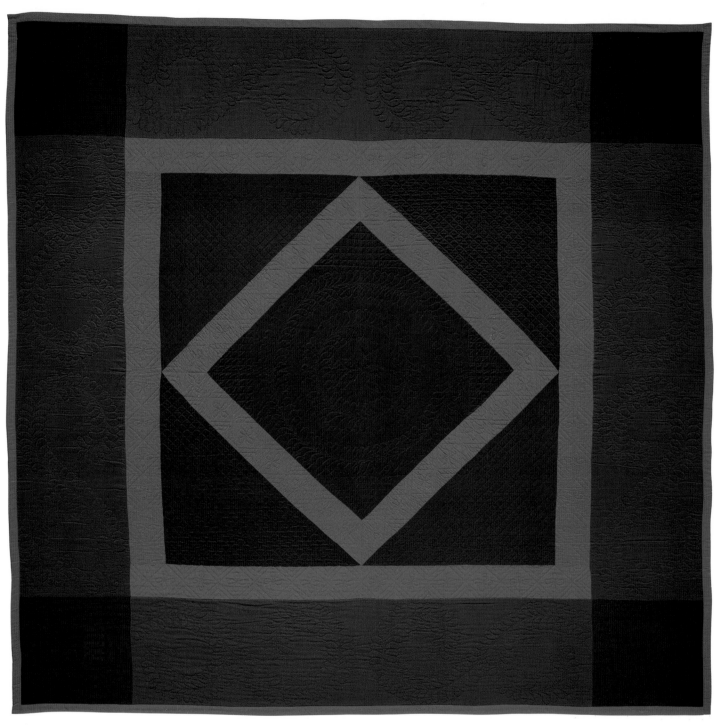

26

26. Center Diamond Quilt

Maker unknown, Amish
Lancaster County, Pennsylvania, about 1910–40
Wool and cotton
Sansbury-Mills Fund, 1973 (1973.157)

27. Sunshine and Shadow Quilt

Maker unknown, Amish
Probably Lancaster County, Pennsylvania, about 1920–40
Wool and cotton
Purchase, Eva Gebhard-Gourgaud Foundation Gift, 1973 (1973.94)

The Amish are followers of Jacob Amman (about 1644–about 1730), an extremely conservative Swiss Mennonite bishop who split with the Mennonite Church in the 1690s because he felt that it did not practice shunning of those who deviated from church rules with enough severity. His followers migrated to the Palatinate region of Germany, but because they were persecuted in Europe for their ascetic beliefs, they immigrated to Pennsylvania in about 1727 at the invitation of William Penn, settling at first primarily in the rich farmland of Lancaster County. In later years, Amish communities spread to other areas of Pennsylvania as well as Ohio, Indiana, and Iowa.

Today, as in the seventeenth century, the Amish attempt to keep themselves at a distance from those leading what they see as a worldly life. They reject those modern conveniences they perceive to be "of the world," such as cars, electricity, indoor plumbing, telephones, television, rubber tires, and buttons. However, they do use sewing machines, albeit treadle-powered ones. Their style of plain dress, a holdover from at least a century ago that serves as a visual boundary to separate them from the rest of the world, is an important factor in the appearance of their quilts. Women's dresses and men's shirts are made in a rainbow of brilliantly hued solid fabrics, and because this cloth is the only type readily available in Amish communities, it is also used to make the vivid and often surprisingly gay quilts we associate with the Amish.

The Center Diamond pattern (catalogue no. 26) is a favorite of the Amish of Lancaster County. Patterns such as Sunshine and Shadow (catalogue no. 27) and Bars (p. 197) are also closely associated with the Lancaster County Amish, who are considered among the most conservative of the Amish communities.

All of these patterns have a central focus, like the quilts we have seen from the period before 1850. Amish dress evolved as a simpler version of worldly costume until about the time of the Civil War; perhaps the conservative Amish of Lancaster County preferred the early nineteenth-century quilt designs as well.

A Center Diamond quilt is made with fairly large pieces of fabric, which are likely to have been purchased specifically with the quilt in mind. The simple composition of a work such as our Center Diamond quilt made it a perfect canvas for the elaborate quilt stitching that is one of the hallmarks of an Amish quilt. This piece has the most accomplished quilting of all our Amish quilts. As with most quilts of this type, there is a star at the very center of the diamond. Eight-pointed stars are the norm, but our star, for some unknown reason, has only seven points. The star is surrounded by two feather wreaths. The narrow red borders are filled with pumpkin-seed quilting, and the wide outer border contains a gracefully curving feather pattern.

The Sunshine and Shadow pattern is made by sewing together small squares of fabric that have been arranged by color to form concentric rings of brightly colored diamonds. These are framed by a wide border, which is often anchored with large square corner blocks. Sunshine and Shadow quilts do not afford the maker as much area for fancy quilting. Usually the small squares are either quilted near each seam, or, as in our example, the squares are simply cross-hatched with diagonal lines of stitching. However, the wide outer border can be decorated with many traditional designs—in this case, feather quilting in a somewhat different composition from that of the Center Diamond quilt's border.

The Sunshine and Shadow pattern may have grown out of the Center Diamond pattern around the turn of the twentieth century. It has often been interpreted outside Amish communities as a representation of the Amish people's belief in life's balances, such as day and night, summer and winter, good and evil, and in the ways of the outside world as opposed to the Amish way of life. Whether this particular quilt pattern has specific meaning to the Amish themselves has never been conclusively proved; it may be that it is favored simply because of its vibrant appearance. Although Sunshine and Shadow is usually thought to be exclusively a Lancaster County pattern, a few documented examples exist from other Amish communities.

27

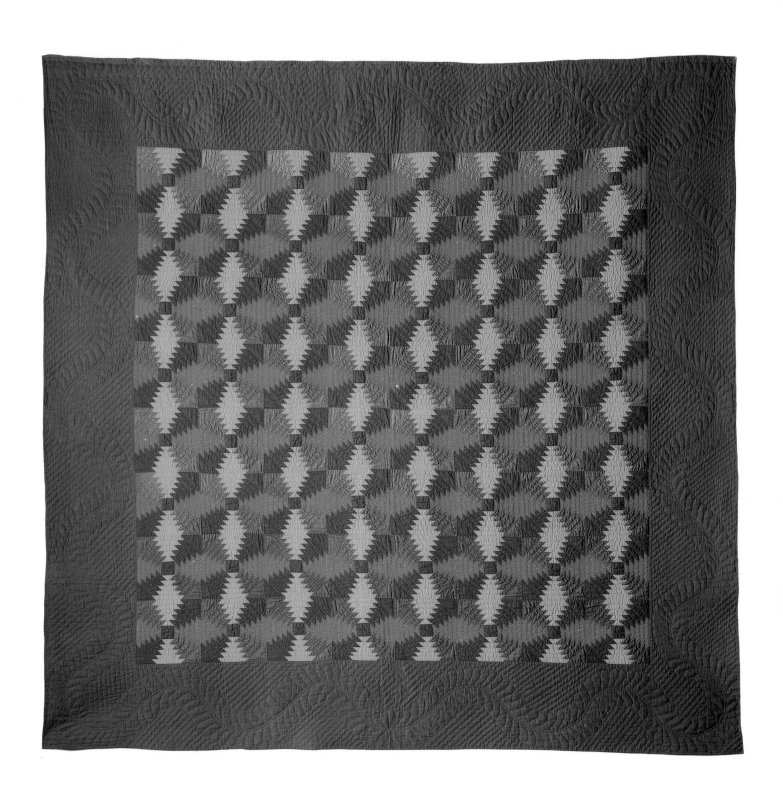

28. Log Cabin Quilt (Pineapple variation)

Maker unknown, probably Amish or Mennonite
Pennsylvania, about 1900–1930
Cotton
Purchase, Mr. and Mrs. George M. Kaufman Gift, 1973 (1973.22)

The Pineapple variation of the Log Cabin quilt is thought to be related to eighteenth-century symbolism, in which pineapples represented hospitality. This Pennsylvania quilt is one of the more literal representations of the pineapple theme, pieced of gold, red, green, and earth-colored brown cotton. In the Pineapple variation of a Log Cabin quilt, the central squares or "hearths" are not a primary element in the design. The central squares of each block in this quilt are cut from the same brown fabric as the border and also as some of the pineapple leaves. In the Pineapple pattern, the central square is not surrounded by four "logs" of fabric, but rather with eight overlapping logs, both parallel with and at forty-five-degree angles to the central square's sides. This pattern, also known as Windmill Blades, can be quite dizzying when pieced with printed fabrics, but when superbly planned, as in this example, it is a pattern of great strength and energy.

Our quilt could have had either an Amish or Mennonite maker. Log Cabin quilts in all variations were popular with both sects, and they demonstrate the distinctive quiltmaking traditions of these two groups. Amish and Mennonite quiltmakers use primarily solid-color fabrics. The visual result of this choice of materials is vividly exemplified by the striking difference in appearance between this quilt of rich bold colors and our Straight Furrow and Light and Dark variation quilts (catalogue nos. 19, 20), which are composed of variously printed wool challises.

29. Squares and Bars Quilt

Maker unknown, Amish
Probably Lancaster County, Pennsylvania, 1892
Wool
Gift of Mr. and Mrs. Stanley Tananbaum, 1973 (1973.124)

This simply designed quilt, pieced from what appear to be home-dyed fabrics, was probably made in Lancaster County. Signed and dated Pennsylvania-Amish quilts are very rare. The embroidered inscription *18 A K 92* at the bottom of the center square makes this one of the few Amish quilts that can be properly documented to the nineteenth century.

When Amish quilts were first discovered by collectors and museums in the 1970s, there was a tendency to date many of them to the latter part of the nineteenth century. As scholarship progressed, however, it became clear that the vast majority of the Amish quilts seen today in collections and publications were made in the first four decades of the twentieth century. Many were thought to be from the nineteenth century because the Amish apparently came to the practice of quiltmaking about fifty years after the height of its popularity in the outside world, employing patterns such as the Log Cabin and the Crazy quilt well after the peak of their use among other quiltmakers.

The golden age of Amish quiltmaking occurred between 1890 and 1940. Quilts from this period are distinguished by their generally dark coloration, fine quilt stitching, and natural fiber fabrics. After 1940, synthetic fabrics and batting changed the look of Amish quilts. Man-made fabrics are often more durable than natural-fiber cloths, and synthetic batting is easier to sew through than the cotton batting of the earlier period. However, these new materials do not enhance a quilt's appearance, since synthetics such as rayon and, later, polyester, have a reflective sheen that affects the depth of the fabric's color, giving it a lighter look. This is easy to spot when a newer quilt is compared with an earlier, more deeply hued wool or cotton quilt. Synthetic batting has more loft than cotton batting, and because of this added thickness, the number of quilting stitches per inch tends to be reduced, resulting in less intricate quilting patterns.

When Amish quiltmakers realized that the outside world was interested in purchasing their quilts, they began to produce them specifically for sale to that market. These are often made to fit modern queen- and king-size beds, an enlargement in overall size that has led to an increase in the scale of many of the patterns. Some new Amish quilts are made in light colors to coordinate with modern interiors, and sometimes they even include printed fabrics. Because of these changes, the distinctive qualities of Amish quiltmaking are rapidly disappearing, making a classic quilt such as this one a treasured example of an almost lost art.

30. Pinwheel Quilt

Maker unknown, Amish
Indiana, 1930
Wool and cotton
Friends of the American Wing Fund, 1988 (1988.128)

Unlike those by the Pennsylvania Amish, quilts made by the Indiana Amish are often initialed and dated. This example is inscribed *J. L.* in quilting on one of the four corner triangles of the central patterned area. Each of the other three corners is stitched with part of the date on which the quilt was completed; clockwise from the maker's initials, the first corner is marked *Jan*, the next, *23*, and the last, *1930*. This is therefore one of the Museum's most recently made quilts. Although it was created well into the twentieth century, it fits comfortably into our collection, since its design is clearly a continuation of a nineteenth-century aesthetic.

Indiana (and other midwestern) Amish quilts are usually quite different in appearance from those of the Lancaster County Amish. A reflection of the more liberal attitudes of the midwestern Amish communities, they are pieced in a great variety of overall patterns, a large number of which have been adopted from the outside world. Many of the quilts have blue or black background fabric. It seems that the makers very often preferred block patterns, set as diamonds rather than squares, the pieced blocks alternating with plain blocks that are decorated with elaborate quilting. The plain blocks in this work are quilted with feather wreaths. It is somewhat unusual that the red inner border and the black outer border are not quilted with separate patterns; instead, the fiddlehead fern motif is quilted through both. The pieced blocks are set so that the left and the right halves of this work are almost identical. This orderly placement seems particularly appropriate to Amish sensibility.

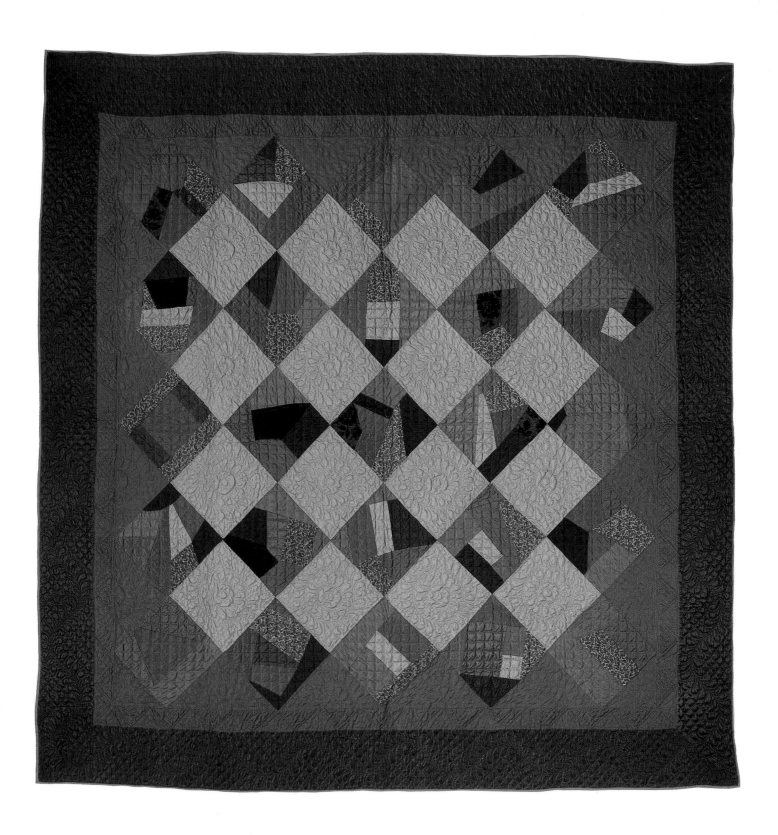

31. Silk Crazy Quilt

Maker unknown, probably Quaker
Pennsylvania, about 1885–1900
Silk, silk velvet, and wool
Purchase, Virginia Groomes Gift, in memory of Mary W. Groomes,
*   1974 (1974.34)*

Unlike the Amish, who live in isolated communities and practice their religion as completely separated from the outside world as possible, Quakers remain in the world and attempt to reform it. This difference accounts for the higher degree of likeness to broader trends in art and design found in objects made by Quakers.

Members of the Religious Society of Friends, or Quakers, as they are more commonly known, first arrived in the American colonies from England in 1656. Although the majority of Quakers were farmers and country people, most were fairly well-to-do. By the middle of the eighteenth century, the Quakers of Philadelphia, many of whom were wealthy merchants, were considered the aristocracy of the city. For a Quaker, affluence posed a problem: how to maintain the important religious virtues of simplicity and equality while enjoying one's wealth. Eighteenth-century observers noted that although the Quakers insisted on simply designed furnishings and clothes, these objects were always made from the finest materials. In women's clothing, this translated into simple, unornamented silk and velvet dresses in muted tones.

The silk quilts associated with the Quakers were a natural outgrowth of the stylish quilted silk petticoats worn by Quaker (and other well-to-do) women in the late eighteenth century (Figure 11). These petticoats were meant to be seen as decorated panels under the split-front skirts of the period. Quilted silk garments were popular in England as early as the middle of the seventeenth century, and many examples of silk petticoats and whole-cloth silk quilts from the early eighteenth century still exist in English collections. The Quakers were English immigrants and followed the traditions of their homeland. Although few eighteenth-century silk bed covers exist in the United States, there are numerous examples of quilted silk petticoats. When this style of dress went out of fashion, the petticoats were often used as sections of bed coverings. Undoubtedly, these attractive works inspired Quaker women to continue to produce silk quilts throughout the nineteenth century, although they evolved from the whole-cloth to the block pieced type.

The Crazy quilt illustrated here was made in the later decades of the nineteenth century, when a wide variety of silks were being pieced into Quaker quilts. In addition to the solid-colored silks in the characteristic Quaker shades of browns, beiges, and grays, the quilt also includes bits of printed silk, as well as cut and uncut velvets. The wool backing and cotton quilting thread are a surprisingly bright red. For unknown reasons, Crazy quilts were popular with the Quakers, although their versions are quite subdued and orderly. The virtuoso quilting, traditional to this group, also sets this work apart from Crazy quilts made by non-Quakers.

The quilt was originally purchased at an auction that took place in Lancaster County. The people whose property was being sold were not Quakers, and therefore it may be supposed that since many Quakers live in the surrounding areas, either this couple acquired the piece at some point or the local auctioneer added the quilt to the sale from another source. The auction was held in 1973, and because all the people concerned are no longer alive, we may never know who made this superb quilt.

Figure 11. Cream and yellow flowered silk dress over quilted petticoat of plain blue silk; trimmed with bobbin lace. Worn by Susanna Saunders Hopkins of Salem, Massachusetts, about 1771. The Metropolitan Museum of Art, Gift of Helen L. Latting, 1936 (36.64.1, 2)

Detail of catalogue no. 31

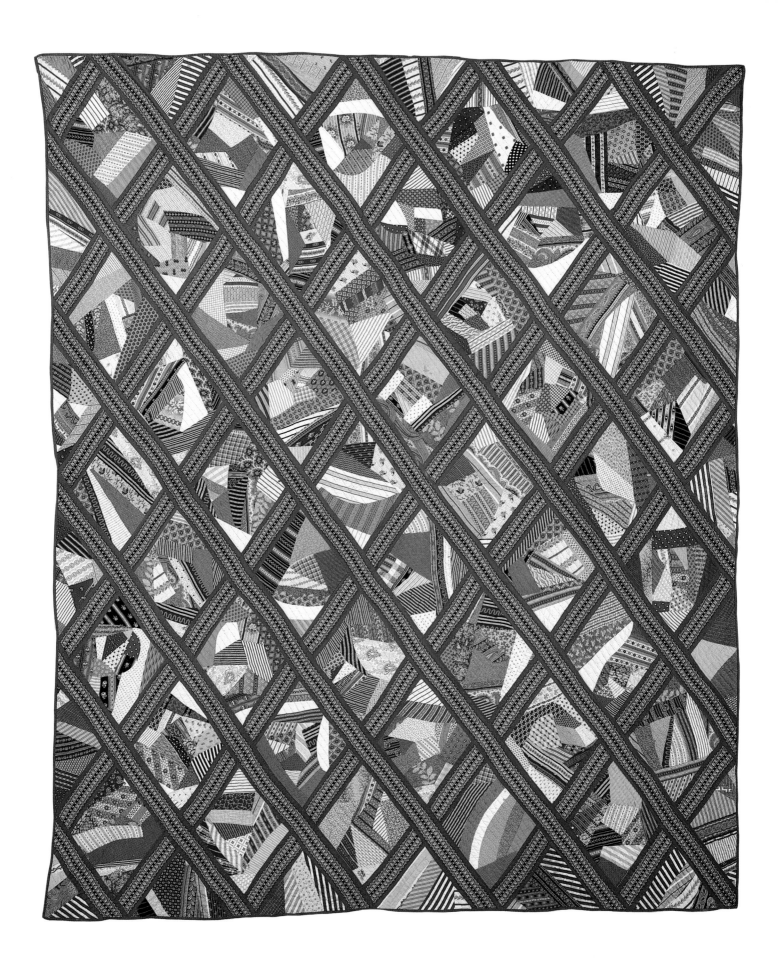

32. Contained Crazy Quilt

Nancy Doughty (about 1790–?)
Probably Maryland, 1872
Cotton
Purchase, Mr. and Mrs. Edward Scheider Gift, 1989 (1989.27)

This unusual work is one of the few Crazy quilts known to have been made during the early 1870s. Although some examples of cotton Crazy quilts have been tentatively dated to the 1860s, our quilt is one of the earliest to be firmly documented. There is an inscription in ink on a piece of striped cotton at this quilt's center: *Made by/Mrs. Nancy Doughty/in the/82nd year of her age/for her friend/Miss Lizzie Cole. A. D. 1872.* The quilt appears never to have been used; when Miss Lizzie Cole received it in 1872, she must have prized the work of her friend Mrs. Nancy Doughty as highly as we do today, and it is likely that she put it away for safekeeping.

Crazy quilts may have been so named because of the random shapes and sizes of the fabric pieces stitched together to form the quilt blocks. This type of pattern had many sources, including the newly rediscovered Japanese art that was so highly influential in Europe and America in the 1870s. Throughout the last two decades of the nineteenth century, silk and velvet Crazy quilts (such as catalogue nos. 33, 34) were the height of fashion. In comparison, this example, with its color scheme of subtle brown and orange printed cottons and contained pattern of pieced diamond-shaped blocks within a grid, has a very different appearance. Unlike the silk and velvet quilts, which were often made from kits, the cotton versions were probably pieced exclusively from scraps of fabric accumulated by the quiltmaker. Although a large number of silk Crazy quilts can still be found today, very few of the earlier cotton versions such as this one survive.

33. Crazy Quilt Top

Maker unknown
New York State, about 1885
Silk, silk velvet, and cotton
Gift of Tracey Blumenreich Zabar, 1989 (1989.66)

The Crazy quilt craze was so widespread in the 1880s and 1890s that it became the subject of comment in the press. The journalists of the trade paper *The Carpet Trade and Review* delighted in publishing anecdotes about men being accosted by young women anxious to snip the silk from the men's hat linings and neckties, to use in piecing their Crazy quilts. An explanation of the origin of Crazy quilts also appeared in the April 1885 issue of *The Carpet Trade and Review* (p. 41):

> "Crazy" patchwork originated in the following manner: A certain titled lady while learning embroidery in an English seminary lost her mind and it became necessary to confine her to a private madhouse. But she still retained her passion for needlework and spent most of her time in uniting pieces of material furnished her from the madhouse scrap-bag. Although unable to perform the difficult stitches of embroidery work, it was noticed that in joining the odds and ends of material given to her she invariably used contrasting or assimilating colors of thread or silk and that nearly every stitch was different from the others. Specimens of her work found their way outside of the asylum and since then millions of women, apparently sane, have found delight in imitating the handiwork of the crazy countess.

Whatever the origin of the use of the word "Crazy" to describe this type of quilt, whether it refers to the cracked or "crazed" appearance of the blocks or to the possibility that a woman might go crazy piecing so many small bits of fabric together, by the mid-1880s, Crazy quilts were so popular that enterprising manufacturers offered them in ready-to-sew kits. Although certainly not all Crazy quilts were made from kits, when one reads through the advertisements of the period, it quickly becomes apparent why so many Crazy quilts are so similar in appearance. The prospective quiltmaker could order complete kits in which there were precut pieces of silk that could be formed into blocks according to instructions explaining how to fit them together properly. Sometimes, the backing fabric was marked like the base of a jigsaw puzzle, showing where to place each piece of silk. Often the silk pieces themselves were stamped with a pattern, such as the outline of a flower, over which one embroidered. If quiltmakers wanted to use their own silk and velvet scraps, they could still order appliqués, commonly machine embroidered, or at least sheets of perforated paper patterns to use in tracing designs onto the patches. There were also iron-on transfer designs and even specially printed sheets of paper with oil-painted pictures that could be transferred onto fabric by pressing the paper

backing with a hot iron. This explains the strangely uniform quality of many Crazy quilts, with their ubiquitous Japanese fans and Kate Greenaway figures. It also makes those Crazy quilts that are not as formulaic seem all the more extraordinary.

It was noted by Mrs. John A. Logan in her 1889 book, *The Home Manual* (p. 288): "Crazy patchwork, to be endurable, must after all, have 'method in its madness.' Distinct artistic skill in the grouping and harmonizing of colors is indispensable to the beauty of the final result." The Crazy quilt top shown here would have been considered a most artistic example. Each block is designed with unusual patterns, and the blocks seem to be composed of real scraps, which in some instances have been pieced together to make fans, chevrons, or geometric figures. There are also some commercially produced elements; the black velvet cats that appear in a number of the blocks, for example, were probably specially purchased. Some of the repeating embroidered motifs, such as the maple leaf, were probably marked first with perforated paper patterns. However, the original aspects of this piece make it stand apart from the run-of-the-mill Crazy quilts that exist in great numbers even today.

Detail of catalogue no. 33

34. Memorial Crazy Quilt

Tamar Horton Harris North (1833–1905)
North's Landing, Indiana, about 1877
Silk, silk velvet, and cotton
Gift of Mr. and Mrs. John S. Cooper, 1983 (1983.349)

The beautifully designed Crazy quilt illustrated here is exceptional for a number of reasons, the most important being that it is one of the few well-documented examples of a mourning quilt. It was made as a memorial after the death of twenty-year-old Grace Gertrude North (May 24, 1856–February 13, 1877), the only child of Tamar and Benjamin North of North's Landing, Indiana.

The quilt's maker, Tamar Horton Harris North, was born on January 25, 1833, near Quercus Grove, Indiana. On May 19, 1852, she married Benjamin F. North (February 7, 1830–January 22, 1877) and went to live with him at North's Landing on the Ohio River. Benjamin North was a well-to-do farmer. During the Civil War, he was a captain of Company C, 83rd Indiana Volunteers, Infantry. After serving for three years, he was discharged because of ill health and returned to North's Landing. We do not know what killed Benjamin and Grace within a month of each other in the winter of 1877.

We assume that Tamar North started work on the quilt soon after her daughter's death. If it was indeed made in 1877, this is a fairly early example of a Crazy quilt. It is pieced of silks and silk velvet, but there are also pieces of cotton and cotton lace. According to family history, North made the quilt from pieces of Grace's dresses, and the types of fabrics used and the unusual additions of bits of lace seem to bear this out. Many symbols of Grace's death ornament the quilt; her name is embroidered at the center, with a calla lily to each side, and in the block to the right, there is a patch inscribed with purple ink that records her birth and death dates. The same block includes a patch that is painted with an angel. Through diaries, it is known that at times of sorrow, sewing seemed to be a great comfort to the nineteenth-century woman.

35. Fan Quilt

Maker unknown
United States, about 1900
Cotton
Purchase, Mrs. Roger Brunschwig Gift, 1988 (1988.24.1)

When trade between the Western nations and Japan opened up in 1854, the influence of Japanese design became evident in many areas of the fine and decorative arts. Japanese design elements are found in Crazy quilts as well as in a particularly Japanesque quilt pattern called the Fan. Fan quilts are most often made of silk and velvet and have much the same aesthetic as Crazy quilts.

The red and white quilt illustrated here was probably made at a somewhat later date than the silk and velvet Fan quilts of the 1880s and 1890s. Quilts made from a combination of red and white cotton were particularly popular in the early part of the twentieth century. However, this example is not a true red and white quilt, since the white background fabric is printed with tiny blue dots. This makes the quilt subtly evocative of America's national colors, in spite of the fact that the center square looks rather like a Japanese flag. The placement of the blocks cleverly reinforces the fan imagery. There are six blocks across and six blocks down; the two central blocks in the outermost row on each side have been paired to form four fully open fans, to which the quiltmaker has added straight handles. The other blocks are composed of identical half-open fans set at angles to each other, and all of the blocks are decorated with fan-patterned quilting that further accentuates the overall design.

36. Alice in Wonderland Quilt

Marion Cheever Whiteside Newton (?–1965)
New York City, 1945
Cotton
Purchase, Edward C. Moore, Jr. Gift, 1945 (45.38)

At the turn of the twentieth century, interest in quiltmaking had slackened considerably. Some people attribute this to the oversaturation that occurred during the Crazy quilt era. But in the 1920s, the American patriotism brought about by the successful waging of World War I revitalized the supposedly colonial practice of quiltmaking, and it continued to flourish through the Depression, when it was considered symbolic of the American characteristics of thrift and self-sufficiency. By the 1940s, quiltmaking was becoming accepted as an art form, and the Metropolitan commissioned this Alice in Wonderland crib quilt to be made for its collection. During the process of appropriating money to purchase the quilt with funds from the Edward C. Moore, Jr. Fund, the money the Museum used at that time for the purchase of objects of modern decorative art, a curator explained why the piece was necessary to the collection (transcript in the Archives of The Metropolitan Museum of Art):

> The Textile Study Room receives constant inquiries about quilting. As we own no examples of contemporary work, this purchase would provide a useful piece for study purposes. In this quilt, the techniques of embroidery, appliqué, and quilting are represented. The drawing is competent, and the subject matter amusing. Mrs. Newton, who designed and made this quilt, is considered one of the outstanding craftswomen in her field.

According to a 1944 article by Mary Anderson in the *New York World-Telegram*, Marion Whiteside Newton ran a successful quiltmaking business, first organized in the 1930s, specializing in children's quilts that were usually appliquéd with storybook themes. Mrs. Newton (whose name was sometimes published as Marion Cheever Whiteside) designed all her quilts at her workshop at 1212 Fifth Avenue, but once the business began in earnest, she did not sew them herself. The above-mentioned newspaper article notes: ''Now Mrs. Newton has streamlined the process. She makes all her own designs. Two assistants transfer them to the fabric squares. Colors of cotton pieces are selected for the appliqués, and the blocks with instructions are sent to her sewers. Back they come to be assembled, filling and backing added, and the quilting and finishing done by specialists.'' Newton's quilt designs were published in magazines such as *McCall's Magazine* and *Ladies Home Journal*, and the latter ran a series on the Storybook quilts in issues from 1949 through 1961. She popularized her work further by marketing ready-to-sew kits. Her more expensive ready-made quilts were sold by special order only through Saks Fifth Avenue.

Because interest has been primarily focused on nineteenth-century quilts during recent years, this quilt has been somewhat ignored. A new appreciation of the quilts of the first half of the twentieth century has arisen, however, and reappraisal of this work reveals it to be among the fresher and more pleasingly designed quilts of its era.

37

37. Doll Quilt

Ella Mygatt Whittlesey (about 1845–?)
United States, 1852
Cotton
Purchase, Mrs. Roger Brunschwig Gift, 1988 (1988.213)

38. Crib Quilt

Maker unknown
Pennsylvania, about 1840
Cotton
Friends of the American Wing Fund, 1989 (1989.255)

In *Godey's Lady's Book*'s January 1835 issue (p. 41), it was suggested: "Little girls often find amusement in making patchwork quilts for the beds of their dolls, and some even go so far as to make cradle-quilts for their infant brothers and sisters." As *Godey's* notes, very young girls were encouraged to attempt patchwork for much the same reason they learned to make embroidered samplers: This type of project taught them the basic needlework skills they would need to run their own homes competently when they reached adulthood. The majority of nineteenth-century women made all their family's clothes and linens, many without the benefit of a sewing machine; therefore, it was never too early to teach a girl how to stitch a straight, secure seam. By sewing a patchwork quilt for her doll, a little girl learned the running stitch, the backstitch, and also probably the hemstitch, which she might use to finish the quilt's edges. Catherine E. Beecher and Harriet Beecher Stowe, in their well-respected book, *The American Woman's Home* (p. 298), suggested the following method of teaching a young girl to sew:

> When a young girl begins to sew, her mother can promise her a small bed and pillow as soon as she has sewed a patch quilt for them; and then a bedstead, as soon as she has sewed the sheets and cases for pillows; and then a large doll to dress, as soon as she has made undergarments; and thus go on till the whole contents of the baby-house are earned by the needle and the skill of its little owner. Thus the task of learning to sew will become a pleasure; and every new toy will be earned by useful exertion.

Learning to sew was probably not always such a pleasure, since a child sometimes had to complete a prescribed amount of daily sewing, often called her "stint," before she was allowed to play. The inscription written in ink on the back of our Chimney Sweep patterned doll quilt (catalogue no. 37) says: *ELLA Mygatt Whittlesey/ AGED SEVEN. Her "stint"/ taught by her Grandmother Elinor Stuart./ 1852* (see detail below). It is likely that the young maker was obliged to finish a Chimney Sweep block each day before she went on to other, perhaps more recreational, activities. Making her quilt required quite a lot of hand sewing for a little girl of seven, and it may have taken her several weeks to do it all. After the pieced blocks were completed, she had to attach them to the plain blocks. Then the quilt had to be filled, backed, quilted, and the edge bound.

The Museum owns a few other small-size quilts in addition to the doll quilt. Our crib quilt (catalogue no. 38) from Pennsylvania is completely hand stitched of red calico and plain white cotton cloth in the difficult-to-piece Millwheel pattern. All such patterns that incorporate curved pieces are particularly challenging to the quiltmaker, since it takes great precision and small, careful stitches to make a curved seam lie flat. Crib quilts are extremely popular with collectors today. Their small size makes them easy to hang as art, and the small-scale patterns are often very attractive. Even the rather worn and faded appearance of these often-washed quilts adds to their appeal; they have been preserved as precious objects, made by a mother to warm her child.

Detail of back of catalogue no. 37

38

39. Strip Quilt

Maker unknown
United States or England, about 1825
Cotton
Bequest of Flora E. Whiting, 1971 (1971.180.125)

The appearance of a Strip quilt is usually very like that of a whole-cloth quilt, even though it is technically pieced. Therefore, this bed cover, which cleverly incorporates many presumably leftover pieces of early nineteenth-century furnishing cottons, has been placed in the whole-cloth section of the book. All these fabrics have large-scale patterns that would not have been as visually effective if the quiltmaker had chosen to piece them into a small-scale pattern. They were manufactured in England during the period between 1815 and 1825; some were quite common and match pieces of the same fabrics in other museums' collections. A few of the fabrics are block-printed, and others are roller-printed. Most of them are not of the finest quality available at the time. Block-printed patterns such as the one showing peacocks and their chicks on the center-strip fabric were often copied from earlier English fabrics. This particular one was copied from a delicately drawn copperplate print, in red on a white linen and cotton cloth, which was originally manufactured in about 1765–75, possibly by the textile printers G. P. and J. Baker, Ltd. The strips on both sides of the center one were cut from another widely used bird pattern, of about 1815. This quilt is a particularly good illustration of early nineteenth-century fashions in upholstery and drapery fabrics. Bird and pillar prints were favorites, and the way the strips are placed mimics the vertical composition of contemporaneous fabric designs. The fabric strips are placed so that they mirror one another, making the quilt symmetrical outward from the center strip.

The quilt could have been made in England, but the coarsely woven white cotton backing, which is typically found on American quilts of the period, may suggest American origins. Another possible indicator of an American provenance is the piece's very simple double-diamond quilting, which covers the entire surface except for the outermost border, which is stitched with a variation of rope quilting. English quilting is often more ornate, incorporating a wider variety of decorative patterns.

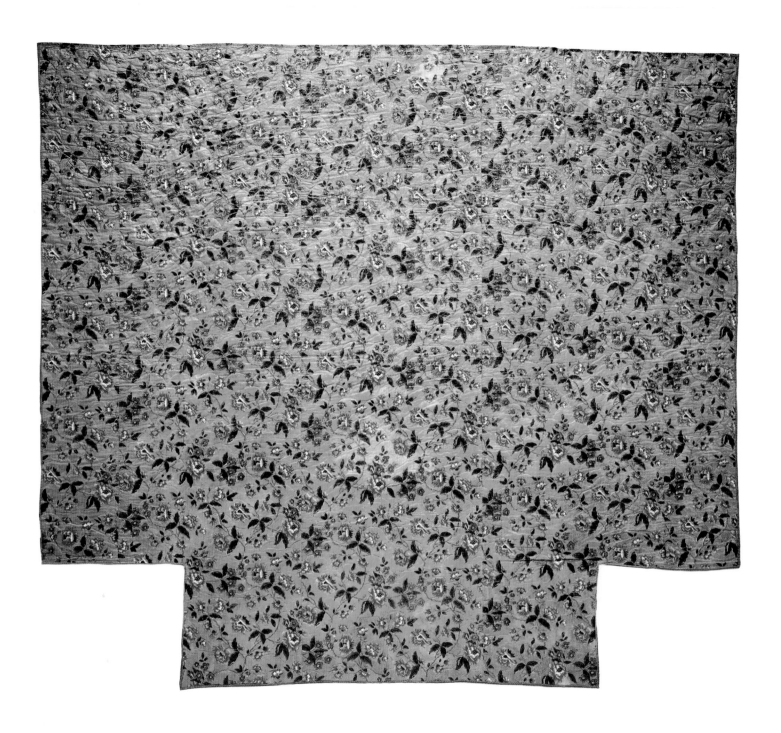

40. Whole-cloth Quilt

Maker unknown
England or United States, about 1835
Cotton
Gift of Mr. and Mrs. Harcourt Amory, 1963 (Inst. 63.7.10)

Although they are often ignored by pieced-quilt admirers, whole-cloth quilts can be important documents of tastes in home furnishing fabrics during various periods, since they incorporate complete lengths of fabric. In addition, the absence of appliquéd or pieced surface patterning sometimes encouraged makers to embellish their quilts with more intricate quilting patterns. This whole-cloth quilt, constructed with a different cotton chintz on each side, falls into the first category. The top, an English fabric manufactured in about 1835, is in a floral trail design, roller-printed in red on a tan blotch ground. The blue, yellow, and green areas are surface-printed with blocks. The fabric on the reverse side, also English, of about 1830, is in a floral stripe pattern of lilies, poppies, roses, geraniums, and passionflowers, roller-printed in red and black (now faded to brown) on what Florence Montgomery, in her authoritative book, *Printed Textiles*, calls a "fancy machine ground." Toward the bottom of the quilt's back (see detail below), there is a small patch of the same floral stripe pattern that is surface-printed with yellow and blue dyes. These dyes have turned the lilies from red to orange and the leaves from black to green. The patch is an example of how manufacturers changed the appearance of the same basic roller-printed fabric in order to give the consumer a variety of choices at little extra cost to the manufacturer. Figure 333 of *Printed Textiles* shows another example, on which the same floral stripe is printed in yet another variation; this time the fancy machine ground has been changed to a pattern of trellis and leaves, while the large flowers remain the same.

Purchasing enough fabric to make a quilt such as this one was probably a considerable investment when compared to the cost of using leftover pieces of furnishing fabrics such as those in our Strip quilt (catalogue no. 39). It is possible that this whole-cloth quilt was made to be part of an entire set of matching chintz bed hangings.

Detail of back of catalogue no. 40

41. Whole-cloth Quilt

Maker unknown
Probably English, about 1790
Cotton
Gift of Mrs. Frederick H. Getman, in memory of her husband, 1945
  (45.145)

This whole-cloth quilt incorporates two English printed cottons, both of about 1785. Although it was owned by a family in New York State, it was most likely made in England and could have been brought over to America by an immigrating family or imported by a merchant soon after it was made. Eighteenth-century business records prove that American merchants ordered bed coverings of all types to be shipped from England, and individuals could order quilts through London agents to be made to their specifications in terms of color choices and fabric types.

The quilt's two printed cottons are well documented. The top is printed with trails of exotic flowers that may have been copied from the designs of Jean Pillement (1728–1808), who published books of ornaments in what was at the time considered to be the Chinese manner. These designs were used by textile printers, painters, and decorators. Although Pillement was French, he spent much of his working life in London, where many of his designs were first published. The fabric was copperplate-printed at Bromley Hall during the period the firm was being operated by Joseph Talwin and Joseph Foster. It is definitively identified by a paper impression of the print that is in The Victoria and Albert Museum's collection of Bromley Hall papers. The paper impression is inscribed *P. 13 Talwin & Foster,* and since Talwin and Foster ran the firm together only between 1785 and 1790, the fabric must have been printed during those years. The backing fabric, made of a less tightly woven cotton, also dates from the 1780s. It is printed with illustrations of Captain James Cook's visits to and death in the Sandwich Islands (former name of the Hawaiian Islands). Some of the scenes are copied from engravings in Captain Cook's books about his travels. He was killed by natives at Owhyhee on February 14, 1779, and the fabric, which served as one of many memorials to him, was probably printed soon after that date.

American quilts are not usually quilted with the patterns seen on this piece; its ornate panels and fan shapes are far more common to English quilts, another reason we assume that the quilt was made in England. Unfortunately, however, we have no conclusive provenance for the work. When an inquiry was made in this regard, one member of the donor's family wrote that Mrs. Getman received the quilt when it was used as a protective packing wrapped around a sewing machine shipped to her by a cousin in upstate New York. Mrs. Getman realized the value of this rare eighteenth-century work and donated it to the Museum.

Back of catalogue no. 41

Opposite: detail of catalogue no. 41

42. Calimanco Quilt

Maker unknown
Possibly New York State, about 1780–1800
Wool
Rogers Fund, 1958 (58.41)

The tops of this quilt and three others in our collection (see acc. nos. 45.107, 62.26, 1980.454; pp. 220, 222, 225, respectively) are made from calimanco, a glazed all-wool fabric. For many years, calimanco quilts were mistakenly called "Linsey-woolsey" quilts. Linsey-woolsey is a cloth usually woven in the home. It has a linen warp and a woolen weft and was used primarily for clothing. It is not clear why calimanco quilts were so often referred to as "Linsey-woolseys" by collectors and quilt historians during the late nineteenth and early twentieth centuries. Calimanco was a professionally manufactured product that, in its fancier guises, was also most often used for clothing. During the eighteenth century, English calimanco was available that was patterned with multiple colors, striped, flowered, or brocaded. However, calimanco quilts found in the United States are generally quite similar to our piece; most examples have single-colored, plain-weave tops that are decorated solely by quilting.

Many calimanco quilts can be dated to the middle of the eighteenth century, but the bold meandering feather vine that enlivens the surface of this quilt became a favorite pattern during the Federal period, suggesting that it was made in the final decades of the eighteenth century. When the Museum purchased it in 1958, the piece was said to have a New York State history, but this has not been confirmed. It is inscribed under the central medallion with the embroidered letters *L M & W D*.

43. Whitework Quilt

Maker unknown
Probably Colchester, New London County, Connecticut, about 1810–15
Cotton
Bequest of Flora E. Whiting, 1971 (1971.180.124)

Both the stuffed and the embroidered types of all-white bed covers were popular during the first third of the nineteenth century. Stuffed whitework quilts such as this one were often made to be included in a bride's wedding outfit. They were particularly prized, possibly because of the sheer amount of labor that went into them. After joining the top and back layers, a young woman outlined the edges of each flower petal or leaf with tiny stitches. Then, she carefully opened spaces in the backing by pushing aside the woven threads of the cloth with her needle. After a tiny area was opened, she inserted small bits of cotton stuffing between the top and back layers in order to produce the raised areas of the design. When an area was stuffed to her satisfaction, the backing fabric was closed by pushing the threads back to their original position. The quilt illustrated here, which is the most beautiful of all the whitework pieces in our collection, must have taken a great deal of time to complete.

The quilt came to us with no provenance. While researching it, we noticed a whitework quilt published in Carleton Safford and Robert Bishop's book, *America's Quilts and Coverlets* (p. 83), that seemed to be almost identical to our piece. It is owned by the Stamford Historical Society in Connecticut. According to their records, that quilt was made by Lucy Foot Bradford (1800?–1875) while she was a young woman living in Colchester, Connecticut. After comparing Stamford's quilt with ours face-to-face, it became apparent that although they were not made by the same person, they originate from a very similar pattern. Patterns, either homemade or professionally printed, were available at this time for this type of fancywork. The similarities were so great that it seemed conclusive that the two pieces had both been made in Colchester, possibly under the tutelage of the same person. Lucy Foot and the maker of our quilt could have taken sewing lessons from the same private needlework teacher, or they could have gone to the same school. There was a well-known school in Colchester called Bacon Academy, established in 1802 to provide free education to all the children of Colchester. But whether this person taught at Bacon Academy or privately, as more evidence turned up, it became clear that there must have been one influential sewing teacher in Colchester during the period between about 1810 and 1820. The confirming evidence came when we found a stuffed whitework dressing-table cover in the Metropolitan's own collection that clearly has many similarities to the two quilts in both technique and design. We were pleased to find that it was made by Sarah Clark of Colchester, Connecticut. Clark was born on March 1, 1796 and died on December 7, 1865. She was married to Eziehiel Williams Parsons, M.D., and she probably made the dressing-table cover when she was a teenager, to carry with her to her husband's house when she married. Although Clark was four years older, her teen years coincide closely enough with Lucy Foot's dates to seem to confirm that our quilt was also made in Colchester at about the same time.

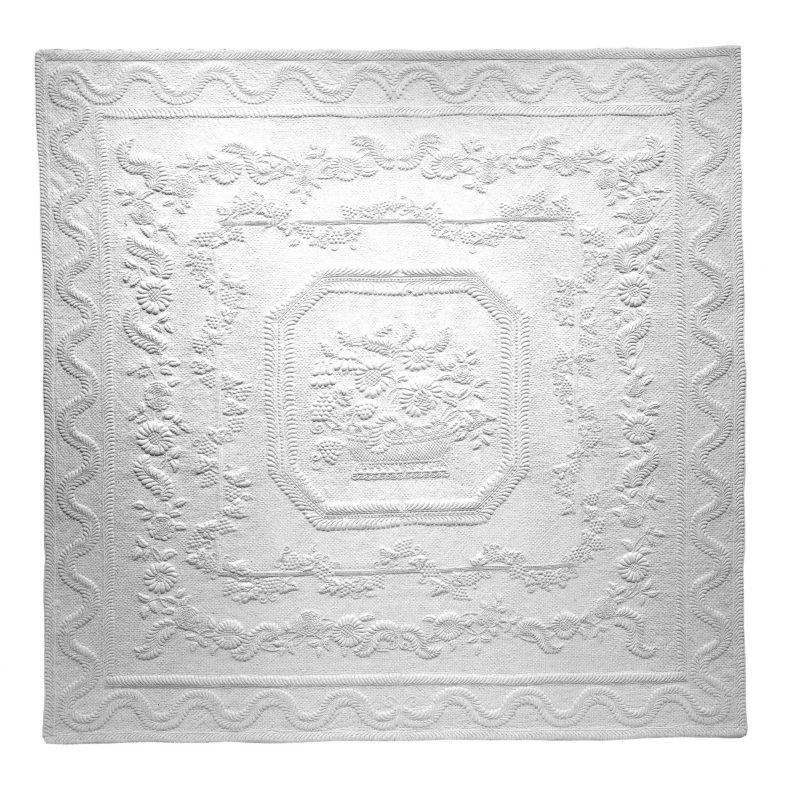

44. Stenciled Coverlet

Maker unknown
Probably New York State, about 1820–40
Cotton
Rogers Fund, 1944 (44.42)

Our stenciled coverlet is a rare surviving example of this type of bed covering, one of the brightest and most charmingly designed of the approximately thirty stenciled bed coverings known today. Like most of that number, ours is neither backed nor quilted. It is composed of a single layer of white cotton cloth, and since it has obviously seen a fair amount of use, we assume that it was never intended to be the top layer of a quilt.

The art of stenciling was practiced extensively during the early decades of the nineteenth century. Homes were decorated with stenciled walls and floors, and furniture was enhanced with birds, flowers, and cornucopias overflowing with fruit. Theorem painting, which entailed stenciling still lifes on velvet or silk, was a favorite activity for students at academies for young ladies. Stenciling techniques were time consuming and painstaking, but little artistic talent was necessary to produce a satisfying finished product. Although some girls may have made their own stencils, professionally designed and cut stencils were available by the mid-1830s.

To create a coverlet such as this one, the maker had to go through a number of careful steps. If she was planning to cut her own stencils, she first chose the motifs with which to decorate the bed cover and then drew the designs either on heavy paper that had been saturated with linseed oil or on cloth dipped in beeswax. A different stencil had to be cut for each part of the design; the maker of our coverlet probably used twelve different stencils to create the central medallion. The base fabric must have been stretched taut by some method in order to ensure the clear definition of each motif. No one has been able to ascertain what type of dyes were used in this kind of work; traditionally, it has been said that the makers prepared their own dyes from homegrown plants, but the intensity of color and opaque surface of the decoration on our coverlet make it probable that commercially prepared dyes or paints were used for this particular piece.

Our coverlet was probably made in New York State, but this type of bed covering was popular throughout New England and the Mid-Atlantic states, and there is even one surprising example with a firm Mississippi provenance. Almost all stenciled quilts and coverlets have been dated to the years between about 1820 and 1840, and our piece fits comfortably into that period.

45. George Washington Quilt

Maker unknown
United States, about 1876
Cotton
Gift of Helen W. Hughart, 1985 (1985.347)

George Washington's image appeared on many textiles, the earliest being eighteenth-century copperplate-printed fabrics. The craze for Washington's image may have reached its height in 1876, when the nation celebrated its Centennial. This quilt's cotton fabric, roller-printed with trompe l'oeil relief busts of the Father of Our Country, was most likely printed in America for the Centennial. Although it has been published as dating from about 1850, the subject matter, the inscription noting *WASHINGTON and INDEPENDENCE/4th July 1776*, and the fact that our quilt is backed with a calico of the browns and reds that seemed so overwhelmingly popular in the 1870s, all make us believe that the fabric, and thereby the quilt, can be dated to about 1876. Another version of the same design also thought to be from about 1876 exists in the J. Doyle Dewitt Collection of the University of Hartford. Their piece of fabric is linen, printed in red, white, and blue. The inscription, which differs slightly from ours, reads: *Union/ Independence/4 July 1776*. The invocation of Union surely means that the fabric had to have been designed at some point after the beginning of the Civil War.

46. Mikado Quilt

Maker unknown
New England, about 1886
Cotton
Gift of Reginald Allen, 1986 (1986.342)

Cotton fabrics printed with imitation patchwork were manufactured in America from around the time of the Centennial in 1876 through the end of the 1880s. The designs on the front and back of this work are among the more amusing prints of this type. The print on the back (see detail below), in imitation Crazy patchwork, illustrates the yachts that raced in the 1886 America's Cup; it has yet to be assigned to a specific printworks. The Mikado print on the front, however, can be documented to an important American printworks. The Museum of American Textile History in Massachusetts was able to identify it in the archives they own from the Cocheco Print Works of Dover, New Hampshire; there is both an engraver's sheet and a sample of the Mikado print, which is identified as style #3286 and dated January 1886. The Cocheco Print Works specialized in bright, inexpensive, and novel printed cottons for the working- and middle-class markets. While the trendsetters of the Aesthetic Movement were seriously considering the influence of Japanese design on Western art, the general public was delighting in Gilbert and Sullivan's 1885 comic operetta, *The Mikado*. Its fame must have spread quickly, because the Cocheco designers' Mikado print fabric was ready within months of the operetta's London debut.

The layers of this simple quilt are attached in the most elementary way. In the manner of many Crazy quilts that have actually been pieced, this work's cotton top, back, and batting are tied through with cotton threads, in this case at the interstices of each "block" on the Mikado side. This carefully placed tying probably means that the Mikado side was originally meant to be the top of the quilt, but the America's Cup side is much more faded and light-bleached, indicating that it lay face up for a long time.

Detail of back of catalogue no. 46

47. Marseilles Quilt

Maker unknown
Probably Manchester, Lancashire, England, about 1780–1820
Cotton
Bequest of Maria P. James, 1910 (11.60.329)

During the later decades of the eighteenth century, the cotton weaving industry in England expanded rapidly. The areas around Manchester and nearby Bolton, Lancashire, produced cotton yardage for various purposes and became well known for two different types of white cotton bed covers. The Manchester weavers made a cloth they called "Marseilles" quilting both in yardage and as bed covers. Woven with a layer of heavy cording between the top and bottom layers, this double cloth was made to resemble fine hand quilting. It is possible that during the eighteenth century, the French port of Marseilles was a center for quilted petticoats and coverlets, and it is assumed that this is the origin of the name given to the Manchester weavers' product. It is known that during the second half of the eighteenth century, American merchants were ordering yardage of Marseilles quilting from England to be used for petticoats and men's summer waistcoats as well as ready-made coverlets. Because of its stylistic similarity to surviving early documented samples of Marseilles quilting, our example can be dated to about 1780–1820. It is hard to be more specific, since Marseilles quilts remained popular throughout the nineteenth century. As late as the 1880s, home decorating manuals were still recommending them for secondary bedrooms. In George A. Martin's 1888 book, *Our Homes; How to Beautify Them*, they were called "neat and washable," and Frank R. and Marion Stockton's 1873 manual, *The Home: Where It Should Be And What To Put In It*, noted that they ranged in price from $2.50 to $6.00. It is likely that the plain white bed covers were considered a welcome change from the complexly patterned Crazy quilts that were then at the height of their popularity.

48. Counterpane

Maker unknown
Possibly New York, about 1810–35
Cotton
Gift of Miss H. Rhoades, 1917 (17.42.2)

The 1845 edition of Webster's *Encyclopedia of Domestic Economy* (pp. 961–62) described the differences between what were then called counterpanes and what were termed Marseilles quilts (see catalogue no. 47):

> *Counterpanes*, evidently a corruption of *counterpoint*, have little protuberances on the surface, dispersed after a certain pattern.
> *Marseilles quilts* are a more elegant kind of bed-quilts, and lighter than common white counterpanes of cotton. This fabric is a double cloth with a third of softer material between, which is kept in its place by quilting done in the loom.

Bolton coverlets, or "counterpanes," were imported to the United States in large quantities starting around the turn of the nineteenth century. Bolton, near Manchester in Lancashire, was the English center of the home industries that produced these all-cotton bed covers. They were woven in one piece on two harness looms that were usually about nine or ten feet wide, either by two weavers sitting side by side at each loom or by a single weaver using a fly shuttle. The pattern was produced by pulling the heavy weft threads up into loops at the appropriate places. The thick cotton design wefts, which resemble candlewicking, were woven into the fabric every few rows in a set proportion (in this example 1:6) to the thinner cotton weft threads. The warp is the same weight as the finer weft threads. The bottom edge of this type of bed cover may have looped inscriptions, which often seem to be the initials of the weaver. Sometimes there are numbers as well, usually indicating the counterpane's original width in one-quarter-yard, or nine-inch increments. Therefore, if a piece is marked 12, like one of the Museum's counterpanes (47.93, p. 241), it means the piece originally measured 108 inches (or 12 x 9 inches) wide. (The piece is now about 103 inches wide, probably due to years of wear and shrinkage from washing.)

Most of the counterpanes in our collection were made in England. The serious study of this type of bed cover is relatively new, but characteristics that distinguish English counterpanes from the few known American examples are coming to light. The first important research on American counterpane weaving was done when Esther I. Schwartz (in her article "Notes from a New Jersey Collector," *Antiques*, October 1958, pp. 330–32) discovered an example inscribed with *Rutgers Factory* woven in the center and *Col. Henry Rutgers 1822* woven in the border. Until Schwartz's discovery, it was assumed that no American factories or weavers in existence during the early nineteenth century were skilled enough to undertake this type of intricate weaving. Schwartz found that the Rutgers factory was one of fifteen cotton factories operating by 1825 in Paterson,

New Jersey. The Rutgers factory owned forty-four looms in 1825, employed one hundred hands, and wove 5,040 yards of fabric a week, and it was not the largest cotton factory in Paterson.

Recent research has revealed that counterpanes were being successfully manufactured in the United States at an even earlier date by smaller concerns. Sandra S. Armentrout has uncovered fascinating information about the work of Eliza Bourne, a professional weaver who lived in Kennebunk, Maine, and produced numerous counterpanes for sale between 1800 and 1820, solely with the help of her large family. She was called a "household manufacturer" by the local press. She had three looms, two of them specifically for counterpane weaving. Her pieces sold for either ten or seventeen dollars each, depending on the grade of quality. (For more on Eliza Bourne, see Sandra S. Armentrout's article in the 1988 Dublin Seminar Proceedings for *House and Home*.)

Our counterpane has a New York City provenance. It belonged to Cornelia H. Hansen and came to us along with her wedding dress. She was married in New York City on the night of the Great Fire of December 16, 1835. The counterpane may have been either part of her trousseau or a wedding present. The eagle and the thirteen stars in the center certainly seem to suggest that the piece is the product of an American manufacturer; the aforementioned Rutgers Factory counterpane bears a similar eagle-and-stars motif. Also, Sandra Armentrout has found the swag border exclusively on counterpanes with American provenances. Because the piece is not inscribed, however, its origins may never be certain.

Detail of catalogue no. 48

49

49. Overshot Coverlet

Maker unknown
Probably Pennsylvania, about 1825
Cotton and wool
Gift of Mrs. Russell Sage, 1909 (10.125.410)

50. Summer and Winter Coverlet

Maker unknown
United States, about 1825
Cotton and wool
The Sylmaris Collection, Gift of George Coe Graves, 1930 (30.120.377)

51. Double Cloth Coverlet

Maker unknown
Possibly New York, about 1825
Cotton and wool
Gift of Margaret and Richard Parrish, in memory of their paternal
*   grandparents, Rebecca and Festus Parrish, 1984 (1984.330.1)*

These three works illustrate the types of non-Jacquard woven coverlets most commonly made during the first few decades of the nineteenth century. The overshot coverlet (catalogue no. 49), woven of orange and blue wool and undyed cotton, is an example of the simplest of the three weaving techniques. The term "overshot" refers to the long passes of supplementary wool weft that overshoot the surface of the plain weave foundation, thereby forming the geometric pattern. Many of the earliest surviving American coverlets are woven in the overshot weave. Our coverlet was woven on a four-harness loom, and the foot end was obviously made to fit around bedposts. The piece could have been made either in the home or in a weaver's workshop. Its provenance is unknown, but it was probably woven sometime quite early in the nineteenth century.

Our Summer and Winter coverlet (catalogue no. 50), dating from about 1825, is a fine example of its type. The origins of the name Summer and Winter are unknown, but it is assumed that it refers to the reversible nature of this cloth. Usually woven in dark-colored wool and undyed cotton, the finished coverlet is primarily dark on one side, light on the other. The term Summer and Winter could refer to the practice of turning over the coverlet when the seasons changed so that the dark side would be on top in the winter and the light side in the summer, or the name could have a more symbolic reference to the dark of winter and the light of summer, or perhaps it relates to both. The weave itself is very similar to the overshot weave; the only difference is that in the Summer and Winter type, the supplementary weft never passes over more than three warp threads at a time and thus produces a denser, more tightly woven fabric. Since Summer and Winter coverlets were generally woven on relatively complex looms with five or more harnesses, they were most likely the products of professional weavers.

Although a West Virginia family owned our double cloth coverlet (catalogue no. 51; for more about that family, see catalogue no. 60), this work is atypical of West Virginia coverlets, which are usually overshot woven; it actually looks more like the type commonly found in New York. Double cloth coverlets were woven by professional weavers on multiple harness looms with two sets of warp threads and two sets of weft threads. The two layers of cloth are woven simultaneously, one above another, with their colors reversed. These layers are joined by interchanging warps and wefts at certain set points in the pattern. The resulting fabric is extremely heavy and warm. The finished coverlet is reversible; the side that is primarily dark wool is usually considered the top, and the light cotton side, the back.

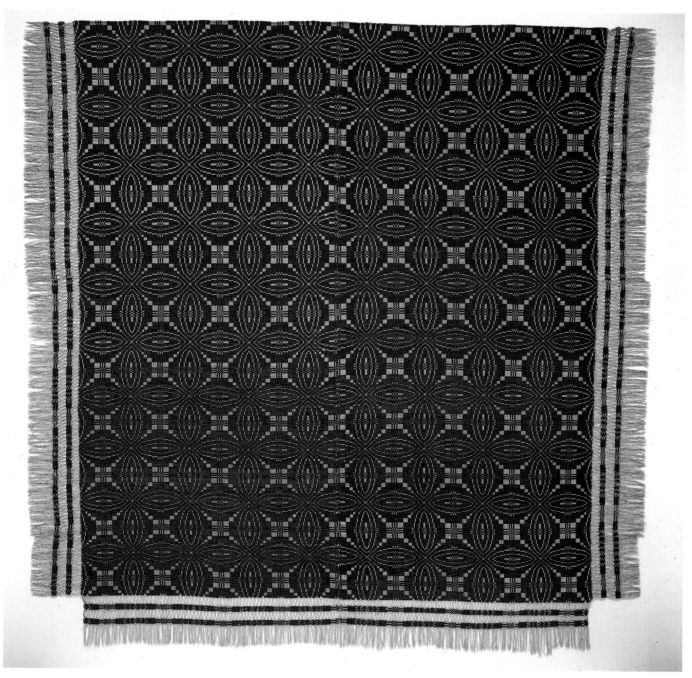

50

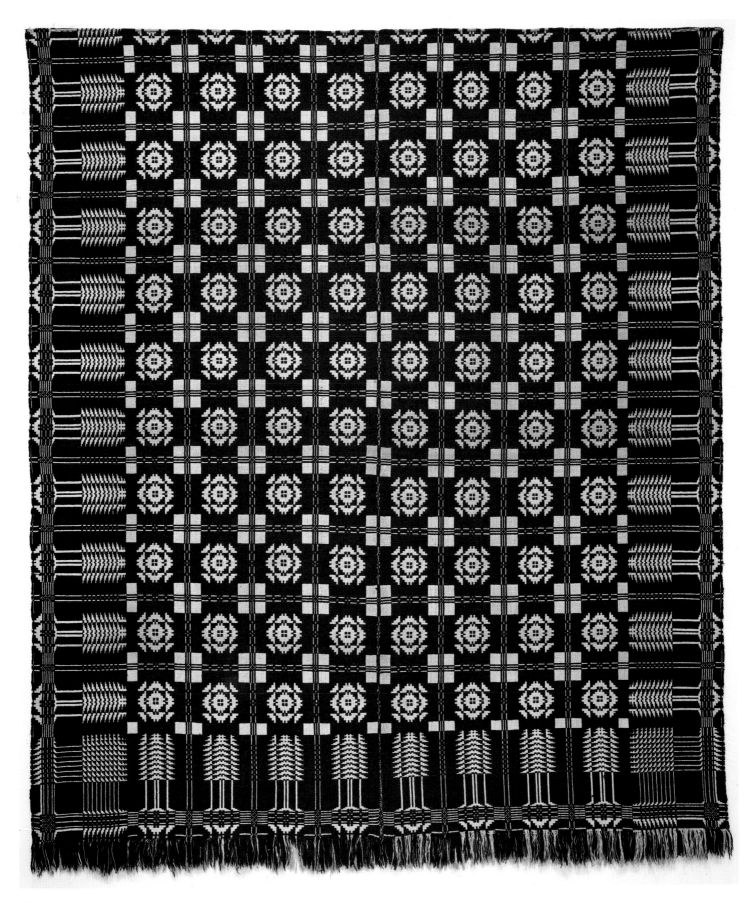

51

52

52. Coverlet

Workshop of James Alexander (1770–1870)
Little Britain, Orange County, New York, 1828
Made for Mary Ann Wood
Cotton and wool
Gift of Roger MacLaughlin, 1967 (67.33)

53. Coverlet

Maker unknown
Probably Ulster County, New York, 1837
Made for Phoebe Tilson
Cotton and wool
Gift of Mrs. Laura Tillson Vail, 1925 (25.127)

At first glance, the Museum's two blue and white double cloth coverlets seem nearly identical. They are both of the type of woven coverlet that traditionally has been attributed to Orange County, New York weaver, James Alexander. Both are patterned with the same medallions, and each has a border that alternates eagles and Masonic symbols. Distinct regional differences exist in the wool and cotton coverlets woven in the United States during the years between 1820 and 1850, when they were at the peak of their popularity, and these two works are good illustrations of the New York style.

The earliest New York weavers who set up businesses in the lower Hudson Valley and Long Island were immigrants from the British Isles. They had been trained in Britain as "scotch carpet" weavers, an apprenticeship that lasted at least seven years. This training in carpet weaving explains both the usual structure and the appearance of New York coverlets. For the most part, they are made of undyed cotton and indigo-dyed blue wool that has been double woven for strength and weight, much like woven carpets of the early nineteenth century. The large medallions in the central fields of these two coverlets look very much like the designs found on English and Scottish carpets of the period. It is important to note that weavers such as James Alexander did not weave coverlets exclusively. They also supplied the community with table linens and floor coverings, which could be woven on the same equipment as the coverlets.

James Alexander was born of Scottish parents in Belfast, Ireland. He trained there as a weaver for seven years before his arrival in the United States in 1798. He settled in Little Britain (near Newburgh) in Orange County, New York, where he farmed and wove fabrics of all types. The New York State Historical Association at Cooperstown owns Alexander's account book, which covers the years from 1798 to 1830. This rare document lists the type of textiles woven by Alexander. In the early 1820s, he began to record that he was weaving "flowert coverlets." Through the course of the account book, it is written that he received 274 orders for this type of work, exemplified by our coverlet (catalogue no. 52). Alexander's account book also lists his clients, what he was to weave for them, and in the case of his coverlets, whose name was to appear in the corner block. Although Mary Ann Wood's name does not appear in the account book, the coverlet made for her (catalogue no. 52) is identical to other documented examples from Alexander's workshop. Alexander coverlets are woven in two strips, which are seamed together. The rather clumsily formed eagles (see detail, p. 145) at the two ends have come to be known as a trademark of Alexander's work. The corner blocks hold simple name and date inscriptions. Alexander hired other weavers to help with his thriving business; under the heading of weaving done by an R. Lockhart in 1828, Alexander listed that thirty-one yards of unspecified fabric were woven for a T. Wood, perhaps a relative of Mary Ann Wood, in July of that year.

Coverlets like the second one illustrated here (catalogue no. 53) have often been attributed to Alexander because of their similarities in pattern to his "flowert" coverlets. Closer examination, however, reveals many differences between the works documented to Alexander and this second type. Small variations within this second group led to the conclusion that they were most likely woven by two or more different weavers, possibly trained by Alexander, who were working in the Dutchess and Ulster County areas, both of which border on Orange County. Woven in a single wide piece, this type of coverlet is distinguished by the legend in the corner block that relates: *AGRICULTURE & MANUFACTURES ARE THE FOUNDATION OF OUR INDEPENDENCE. JULY 4*. A number have been found that are also inscribed with the year 1825 and the name of General Lafayette, who toured America during that year. This variation of the non-Alexander type, for the most part dated between 1825 and 1830, are further distinguished by the appearance of three small figures hidden in the border: A monkey and a deer or goat sit at the feet of the eagles on the narrow ends, and a small man appears at the bottom of the Masonic columns. The names found on this type of coverlet have all been traced to Dutchess County, usually around Poughkeepsie and Fishkill, and it is thus possible that there was one weaver in that area making this small-figured type. There is a second distinct group within the Agriculture and Manufactures type of coverlet, into which our example falls. These works bear the same inscription but are usually dated somewhat later in the 1830s, and their borders contain no small figures. The 1830 Census reveals that Phoebe Tilson, for whom our coverlet was made, lived in Ulster County. It is therefore highly probable that there were at least two other weavers in neighboring counties who made variations of Alexander's original design.

Our second blue and white coverlet (catalogue no. 53) was most likely woven on a hand loom with the assistance of a Jacquard mechanism, the invention responsible for the flowering of coverlet weaving in this country during the second quarter of the nineteenth century. Invented in France in 1804 by Joseph-Marie Jacquard (1752–1834), it enabled a weaver, working without the help of assistants, to produce intricate woven designs of almost any type. The first documented use of the Jacquard mechanism in America was in either 1823 or 1825, by William Horstmann, a Philadelphia manufacturer of coach lace. There is some speculation, however, that the mechanism may have been fitted for a coverlet or rug loom at about the same time, perhaps in New York. Since the Jacquard mechanism had not yet been imported to America in the early 1820s, when Alexander started weaving his "flowert" coverlets, he must have made them on a drawloom. This meant employing a drawboy to pull separate cords after each throw of the shuttle, which controlled the raising and lowering of warp threads necessary to produce the figured pattern. It was a complicated and time-consuming process when compared with the relative ease of weaving fancy patterns with the aid of a Jacquard mechanism.

53

The Jacquard mechanism is attached to the top of the loom frame and is activated by a single treadle. The principle behind it is very much like a keypunch system: The mechanism "reads" punched cards that tell the loom which individual warp threads are to be raised or lowered. One card is punched for each weft in the pattern; all the cards are then laced together and placed over a four-faced cylinder. With each depression of the treadle, the cylinder turns and presses the pattern card against a group of long needles. These needles read the card; if there is a hole punched, the warp thread should be raised; if there is no hole, the warp thread should be lowered. Each needle is attached to a vertical hook, which is connected to a heddle through which each individual warp is passed. The cards are stitched together in a closed chain, so once the initial pattern motif is completed, the design will continue to be repeated. Weavers could punch their own designs on cards or purchase the cards prepunched. The Jacquard mechanism was a major step toward completely automated weaving. It saved the weaver time and the need to hire help, since the warp threads no longer had to be pulled by hand. Most importantly, with the introduction of the Jacquard mechanism, the client was guaranteed a far greater choice of novel designs.

Detail of catalogue no. 52

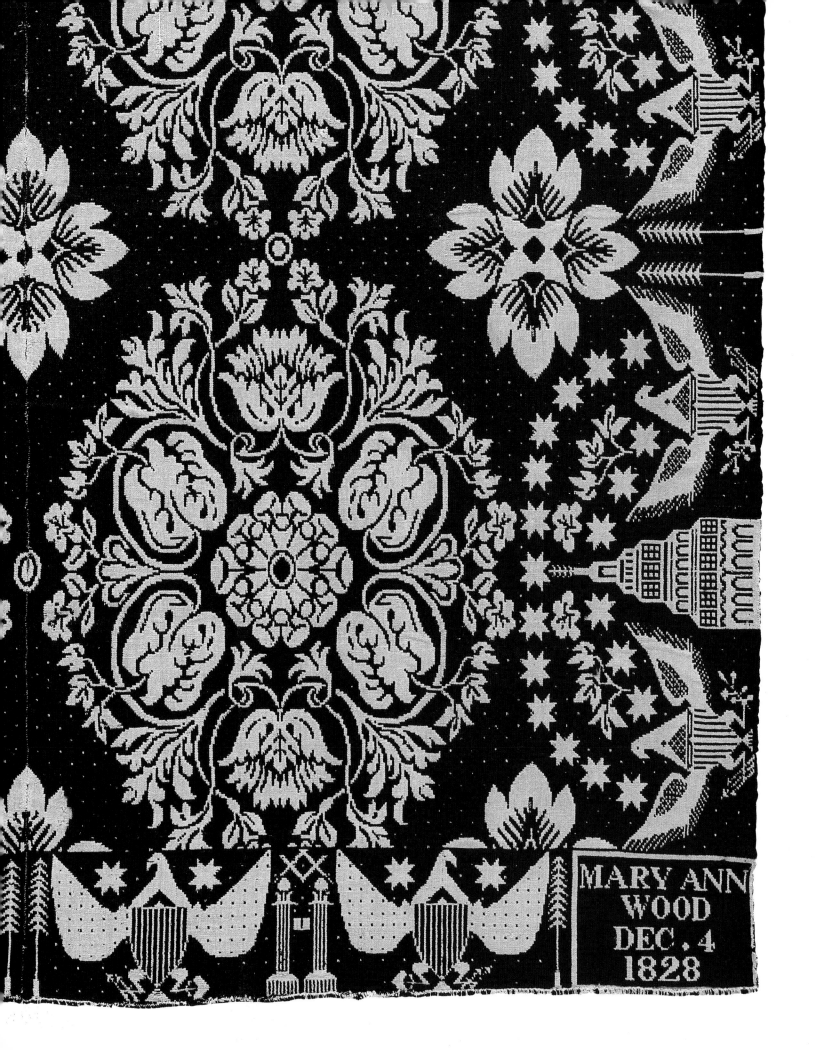

MARY ANN
WOOD
DEC. 4
1828

54. Coverlet

David Daniel Haring (1800–1889)
Tappan Road, Harington Township, Bergen County, New Jersey, 1834
Made for Sarah Ann Outwater Verbryck (1812–?)
Cotton and wool
Purchase, Mrs. Roger Brunschwig Gift, 1988 (1988.127)

55. Crib or Doll Coverlet

Probably David Daniel Haring (1800–1889)
Bergen County, New Jersey, about 1832–38
Made for Rachel Blauvelt (1818–1899)
Cotton and wool
Purchase, Mrs. Roger Brunschwig Gift, 1989 (1989.30)

56. Coverlet

Maker unknown
Rockland County, New York, or Bergen County, New Jersey, 1836
Made for Garret I. Smith
Wool
Purchase, Dr. and Mrs. Kenneth H. Fried Gift and Friends of the
    American Wing Fund, 1982 (1982.366)

David D. Haring (1800–1889) is the best documented of the New Jersey coverlet weavers. The Museum owns three coverlets from the Bergen County area where Haring worked: one signed by him, one attributed to him, and one made by a weaver familiar with Haring's work, or perhaps even trained by him. Haring was born in New Jersey and was a member of a large extended Dutch family that settled in the Bergen County area in the eighteenth century. His work and that of the few other known Bergen County weavers of the period differ in appearance from the coverlets produced during the same years by New York and Pennsylvania weavers. Bergen County coverlet motifs, which are derived from a combination of traditional Dutch designs and symbols of the new American Republic, are quite distinctive, and the coverlets are always double cloth in structure. In addition, it seems that they were woven in only two color variations: dark indigo blue wool and undyed cotton (or occasionally undyed linen) or, in the case of the less common all-wool coverlet, dark and light blue indigo-dyed wool. Haring was the most prolific coverlet weaver in the area, and it is probable that the other weavers who adopted his characteristic motifs either wove with him in his workshop or were trained by him and then went out on their own. The best-known weavers of related coverlets are I. Christie (whose early pieces are practically identical to Haring's) and Nathaniel Young.

Works exist from the years 1832 to 1835 that are signed with Haring's name, initials, or his trademark corner block depicting a rose with four leaves. Our

55

Haring coverlet (catalogue no. 54) is signed *(David D Haring) TAPPAN*. The word *TAPPAN* that Haring inscribed on some of his works with his name refers to Tappan Road in Harington Township, New Jersey, where he lived, rather than to the neighboring town of Tappan in Rockland County, New York. Our piece was made in 1834 for Sarah Ann Outwater, who was born on March 27, 1812. She was the daughter of Dr. Jacob Outwater and Elizabeth Haring Outwater and was David D. Haring's second cousin once removed. Although the coverlet may have been meant to be part of her wedding outfit or trousseau, it was not until four-and-a-half years after it was woven that she married James Verbryck on June 14, 1838.

Unsigned coverlets from the years between 1830 and 1837 have been attributed to Haring. Among these is our rare crib-size coverlet (catalogue no. 55). Marked with the initials *R. B.*, it was acquired from a descendant of Rachel Blauvelt (1818–1899), another cousin of David D. Haring, who, according to family history, was the coverlet's original owner. Her descendants assumed that it had been made to celebrate Rachel's birth in 1818, but all documented coverlets of this type were woven in the 1830s. Although this coverlet most closely resembles the coverlets woven by Haring in the early 1830s, it is tempting to surmise that it was made as a wedding gift when Rachel married Peter T. Haring on May 4, 1838. It has also been theorized that because of the coverlet's diminutive size (31¼ × 30½ inches) and somewhat awkward composition, it may have been made as a plaything for Rachel at an earlier date, perhaps as a covering for her dolls.

The final coverlet in this group (catalogue no. 56) is woven completely of wool, which has been dyed two shades of indigo blue. The maker has not been identified, although a number of weavers in the area made all-wool coverlets, including Haring, whose motifs are the same as many in this piece. However, the work is not signed by Haring, and his two best-known trademarks, a rose with four leaves and a rooster standing on an egg, are missing from it. Instead, each corner block in this piece has a sunflower, a trademark that has not yet been identified. It is possible that this coverlet is the work of a New York State weaver, since it was made for Garret I. Smith, and Smith was a common name at this time in the towns of Piermont and Tallman in Rockland County, New York. These towns border the area of Bergen County where Haring wove. Unfortunately, Smith is such a common name that we have not yet been able to identify the man for whom this coverlet was produced.

57. Coverlet

Peter Leisey (1802–1859)
Cocalico Township, Lancaster County, Pennsylvania, about 1835–50
Cotton and wool
Rogers Fund, 1914 (14.22.1)

58. Coverlet

Absalom Klinger (1817–1901)
Millersburg, Berks County, Pennsylvania, 1846
Cotton and wool
Gift of Mrs. James J. Rorimer, 1989 (1989.264.1)

Bold patterning and intense colors are characteristic of Pennsylvania Jacquard coverlets such as these two works. Unlike the British carpet weavers who immigrated to New York, the German weavers who settled in the southeastern portion of Pennsylvania were professional linen weavers. In addition to bed coverings, their wares included sheets, pillowcases, and towels. The earliest known examples of Pennsylvania-German linens and blankets are brightly colored and patterned with stripes, checks, and plaids, in accordance with the traditions brought over from Germany.

A number of differences distinguish coverlets made in Pennsylvania from those made in the neighboring states of New York and New Jersey. While the New York coverlets are usually "free" double cloth, in which the two layers of fabric are woven together only at spaced intervals, Pennsylvania weavers adopted a technique called tied *Biederwand* (sometimes they also used a plain *Biederwand* weave), which produces a double cloth fabric in which the two layers are completely tied together in the weave, forming what seems to be a single layer of fabric. This technique is similar to damask weaving, which was undoubtedly familiar to weavers who made a portion of their living by producing table linens. It is this tied *Biederwand* weave that gives the background of Pennsylvania coverlets their distinctive vertically ribbed appearance. The most immediately noticeable difference between Pennsylvania coverlets and those made in New York and New Jersey is the Pennsylvania weavers' delightful use of many different colored wools in a single coverlet. While some of the more staid examples were woven in only two colors, most often either in red and white or in blue and white and less often in combinations like our blue and red example (catalogue no. 57), the majority of Pennsylvania coverlets are striped with at least three colors of wool. Some are known that were woven with as many as five variously colored wools. Traditional motifs such as stylized pairs of birds flanking a bush, tulips, and vases of flowers, all of which are typical in German folk art, also set these coverlets apart. Finally, while New York coverlets are usually totally without fringe and those from New Jersey often have fringe only at the foot of the piece, Pennsylvania coverlets have fringe on three sides, with only the head end left plain.

Our two works are somewhat atypical examples of the Pennsylvania Jacquard type. The red and blue coverlet (catalogue no. 57) was woven between

58

1835 and 1850 by Peter Leisey (1802–1859). Not all that much is known about Leisey; he was born in Pennsylvania and was listed in the 1850 United States Census as a farmer in West Cocalico Township, Lancaster County. Other signed examples of his work are known, but none are dated. In this coverlet, woven in two panels and seamed at the center, Leisey created a particularly strong composition by using blue cotton threads for the coverlet's background instead of the more typical undyed cotton. Usually, this blue thread was added only at intervals as a supplemental warp with which the weaver tied down the weft threads. It is the strong contrast between the blue cotton ground and red wool wefts that makes this work of only two colors so highly decorative.

Absalom Klinger (1817–1901), the maker of our second coverlet (catalogue no. 58), was also born in Pennsylvania. He learned to weave from Daniel Bordner of Millersburg (now Bethel) in Berks County. It appears that he numbered all of his coverlets: The earliest known example is number 1,499, which was woven in 1843, and the latest is 2,003, made in 1855. Klinger's numbering system gives insight into the total output of coverlets a successful weaver might produce per year and per career. If Klinger continued to weave until about 1870, when the fashion for woven coverlets finally came to an end in Pennsylvania, he could have produced more than 2,600 coverlets in his lifetime. Our example, made in 1846, was woven in a single wide panel. Its swirling urn pattern illustrates the trend that progressed during the 1840s toward larger field motifs. The stripes, in red and two shades of blue, do not relate all that well to the woven pattern, but the freshness of the colors and unusual design add great appeal to the coverlet.

59. Coverlet

Possibly Mrs. Hicks
Probably Ohio, about 1850
Wool
Rogers Fund, 1956 (56.113)

This intriguing Jacquard coverlet was probably woven in Ohio sometime around 1850. Only one other example decorated with this charming pattern of exotic and domestic animals is known, and although it, too, is supposed to have been woven in Ohio, neither that piece nor ours has a firm provenance. Ohio was on the natural migration route west for Pennsylvania-German weavers who were looking for new territories in which to sell their products, and it was also the destination of almost equal numbers of weavers from Great Britain and Germany who arrived in this country in the 1830s and 1840s. For these reasons, Ohio coverlets often blend characteristics of both New York and Pennsylvania pieces. Our animal coverlet, which was originally fringed on three sides, has a pattern, color scheme, and corner trademark closely related to Pennsylvania coverlets, but it was woven using the same type of double cloth technique found in New York examples. Interestingly enough, it is made completely of wool, like our coverlet from the New Jersey area (catalogue no. 56).

The coverlet was purchased for the Museum's collection in 1956. Along with it, the vendor sent a letter that states: "It was given to me by Mrs. Bertha Ritter, who recently died at the age of 82. The coverlet was woven in Ohio by her grandmother—a Mrs. Hicks" (Archival files, American Decorative Arts Department, The Metropolitan Museum of Art). Although it is more likely that the coverlet was made for Mrs. Hicks rather than by her, there is a small possibility that she did indeed weave the piece. Professional women coverlet weavers are not totally unknown, but the more common role of women was in the preparation of the wool, spinning and dyeing it, for instance, before it was given to the professional weaver to be transformed into a coverlet. This may have led to the misconception held by many families that Grandma actually wove the finished product. Only one woman, Sarah LaTourette of Indiana, can be fully documented as a professional weaver of Jacquard coverlets.

60. Coverlet

Maker unknown
Possibly Indiana, about 1850
Cotton and wool
Gift of Margaret and Richard Parrish, in memory of their paternal
grandparents, Rebecca and Festus Parrish, 1984 (1984.330.2)

Figure 12. Photograph of Rebecca Cunningham Parrish (1846–1938) and Festus Parrish (1840–1938), previous owners of coverlet (catalogue no. 60). The Metropolitan Museum of Art, Gift of Margaret and Richard Parrish, in memory of their paternal grandparents, Rebecca and Festus Parrish, 1984

This coverlet, woven in about 1850, is a good illustration of the close relationship between double cloth coverlets and carpets. It has already been noted that many coverlet weavers also made carpeting, since both items could be woven on the same type of loom. Our coverlet looks as though it was woven on a loom equipped with Jacquard cards punched for a patterned carpet. Mid-nineteenth-century flat-woven strip, or ingrain, carpeting was often decorated with repeating lozenge-shaped figures such as the ones found on this work. The fringes, however, are proof that the piece was clearly meant to be a coverlet.

Our work was the property of Rebecca Cunningham Parrish (1846–1938) and her husband, Festus Parrish (1840–1938), lifelong residents of Marion County, West Virginia (Figure 12). Festus was a schoolteacher and a farmer, and the couple and their son lived in a house Festus built for them. Festus and Rebecca were happily married for more than seventy-two years and died within a few months of each other.

Determining where this coverlet, and another that also belonged to the Parrishes and came to the Museum with it (see catalogue no. 51), were manufactured is a somewhat confusing matter. According to family history, the coverlets belonged to either Rebecca's or Festus's parents. Festus's family settled in West Virginia in the 1780s, and Rebecca's family seem to have been early West Virginians as well. According to their grandson, one of the coverlet's donors, the only time the couple traveled was when they went to Wheeling, West Virginia, for their honeymoon in 1865. Our blue and white geometric double cloth coverlet (catalogue no. 51) looks very much like coverlets woven in New York, and the coverlet illustrated here bears a strong resemblance to pieces woven in Indiana. West Virginia coverlets in the middle of the nineteenth century were more likely to be of the overshot type, usually made in the home. How did Festus and Rebecca come into the possession of two professionally woven coverlets that bear no resemblance to the type of coverlet generally made at the time in West Virginia? Perhaps Rebecca's or Festus's parents traveled west at some point and purchased the coverlets, or maybe relatives living in other states sent the pieces as gifts. However Rebecca and Festus came to own these coverlets, given to the Museum in their memory by their grandchildren, the fine quality of these pieces makes them welcome additions to our collection.

61. Coverlet

Maker unknown
Made for Hannah Mariah Shelden (about 1824–?)
Washington Hollow (Dover District), Dutchess County, New York,
*   1844*
Cotton and wool
Gift of Hazel L. and Saidie E. Scudder, 1986 (1986.175)

As the 1840s passed, the patterns that were used to decorate Jacquard coverlets changed. Throughout the 1820s and 1830s, the designs were usually composed of repeating units. From the 1840s through the 1870s, patterns were more likely to be focused on one large central motif. This change may have come about because larger looms on which a coverlet could be woven in a single wide panel were more readily available by the late 1830s, and the fly shuttle was in regular use. Although coverlets dated as early as the 1820s have been found that were woven in a single panel, until as late as the 1850s, many weavers continued to use a narrow loom, which produced a coverlet of two narrow panels that had to be seamed in the center. This use of the older type loom may have been extended because a narrow loom took up half the space in the weaver's workshop. It was certainly more versatile; in addition to coverlets, the narrow loom could also be used to weave the thirty-five-inch-wide strip carpet that was the standard of the day. However, wide looms may have encouraged weavers to attempt large centralized patterns because wide-loom coverlets did not have to be matched at the center. The weaver of this particular work knew the dictates of fashion and attempted to achieve the effect of wide-loom coverlets while still weaving on a narrow loom. The new taste in decoration that occurred in mid-nineteenth-century America also contributed to the change in coverlet motifs. The subdued and dignified qualities of classical decoration had been highly admired during the early decades of the nineteenth century, but by mid-century, flamboyant naturalistic patterning had come into favor. The type of design on this flowered coverlet, for example, was the height of fashion when the piece was made in 1844, and is very different in appearance from that of our New York State coverlet (catalogue no. 52) that was woven sixteen years earlier.

A weaver's ability to provide this type of up-to-date product was primarily dependent on whether or not he could purchase prepunched cards for his Jacquard mechanism. Although many weavers designed their own patterns and punched their own cards, prepunched cards were available through suppliers in the major East Coast cities. By the 1840s, it seems as though more and more weavers were taking advantage of the ready supply of new patterns, and this coverlet's design and that on the 1846 piece woven by Absalom Klinger of Pennsylvania (catalogue no. 58) were most likely produced by prepunched cards. This change and the migration of weavers farther and farther into the American West as well as north to Canada make it harder to distinguish regional pattern characteristics after the late 1830s.

A series of clues has made it possible to identify Hannah Mariah Shelden, for whom the coverlet was made. The coverlet has many attributes that point to

New York State manufacture: the double cloth structure, the simple red and white coloring, and the absence of fringe. Although no modern maps show a town of Washington in New York State, the donor said that the piece may have belonged to a relative who lived in Dover Plains, Dutchess County, New York. It was ascertained that there was once a town near Dover Plains called Washington Hollow. Since the coverlet was woven in 1844, both the 1840 and 1850 United States Censuses were checked for Sheldens. In the 1850 Census, there was an entry for a Shelden family, in what was called the Dover District of Dutchess County. In 1850, Hannah Shelden was twenty-six years old and married to a farmer named Harrison Shelden, age thirty-five. They had three children living in the household: a nine-month-old infant, a two-year-old, and a thirteen-year-old, who was likely hired help. It is quite possible that Hannah Shelden could have married in 1844, when she was twenty, and that the coverlet was made as a wedding gift.

Detail of catalogue no. 61

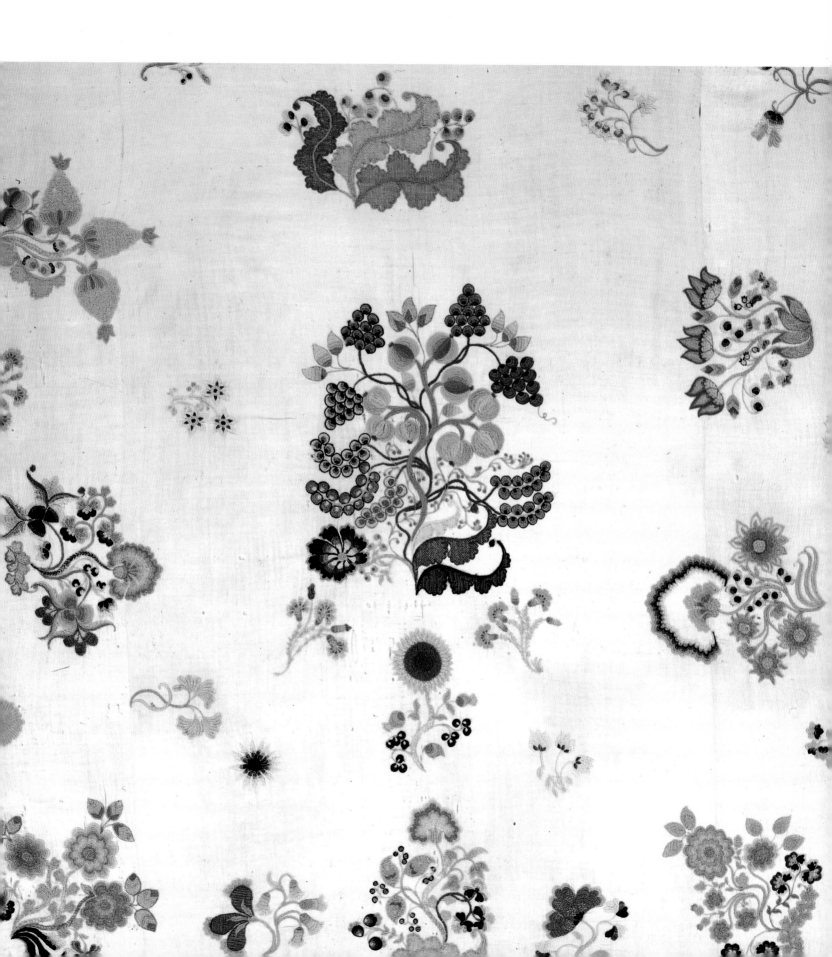

62. Bed Rug

Maker unknown
Probably New London County, Connecticut, 1809
Wool
Rogers Fund, 1913 (13.207)

63. Bed Rug

Maker unknown
Colchester, New London County, Connecticut, 1796
Wool
Rogers Fund, 1933 (33.122)

Bed rugs (referred to as "ruggs" during the late eighteenth century) are completely home-manufactured products. The wool yarn pile is needleworked (not hooked, as was once assumed) in running stitch on a base of handloomed wool or linen. Most often, the base is a wool blanket, the surface of which is entirely obscured by embroidery. All the wool used for making bed rugs such as our two examples was most likely shorn from local sheep. The fleeces were then washed, carded, spun, and dyed by the rug maker.

Although there are a few extant bed rugs that have been embroidered with stitches that lie flat to the surface of the base, the majority have a looped pile that may have been either clipped or left uncut. Both of our bed rugs have cut pile faces. One of them (catalogue no. 63) has some random loops left uncut: The unevenness of the surface seems to indicate that the loops were made without the aid of a reed to keep them at a uniform height and that the surface was clipped with a small scissors or blade.

The bold, overscaled patterning of the typical bed rug is unlike most other embroidered bed coverings of the eighteenth and early nineteenth centuries. The need to create a design that would be effective when made into pile as well as the thickness of the sewing yarns contributed to the use of large motifs and to the pleasing appearance of the end result. The central motif of a bouquet of flowers growing from an undersized urn can be traced to the influence of the image of the Tree of Life commonly found on Indian palampores. The Tree of Life design inspired many quilt and coverlet makers (see catalogue nos. 1, 2), yet it was never used with such vigor as it was on bed rugs.

62

63

Both our bed rugs are thought to be from Connecticut. One (catalogue no. 63) was acquired from the Jonathan Deming house in Colchester, New London County, Connecticut. Unfortunately, our other bed rug (catalogue no. 62) came to the Museum with no history, but it strongly resembles a bed rug in the collection of the Wadsworth Atheneum that has a firm Lebanon, New London County, provenance. The majority of bed rugs have been traced to Connecticut, but they were made throughout New England, and examples are known that range in date from the 1720s to the 1830s.

64. Embroidered Blanket

Henriet Tyler
Connecticut River Valley area, Connecticut or Massachusetts, 1822
Wool
Lent by Elizabeth Ward (L1925)

The few existing examples of this type of wool-embroidered wool blanket usually have family histories that attribute them to makers in Connecticut, Massachusetts, or New York State. Our piece was signed and dated 1822 by its maker, Henriet Tyler, but we don't know exactly where she lived.

Embroidered blankets such as this one are as rare as bed rugs, and the two often have many characteristics in common. (For comparison, see catalogue nos. 62, 63.) Our blanket's central pattern of meandering floral vines with a surrounding paisley border is similar in composition to some of the later heavy pile examples. Like bed rugs, this piece has a handwoven wool blanket as its base; however, unlike bed rugs, the surface of the blanket, which is made of three lengths of fabric seamed together, is not completely obscured. Henriet Tyler embroidered this blanket with brightly colored wool yarns in backstitch, cross-stitch, buttonhole stitch, satin stitch, and French knots. In conception, this type of bed covering seems to be a cross between two earlier forms: pile bed rugs and wool-embroidered linen bed hangings. However, some of the embroidered design elements demonstrate a new awareness of Federal-style decoration. The outer floral vines, for example, are in the process of turning into a tassel-and-swag border. This motif was common in high-style Federal furniture during the earliest part of the nineteenth century; it gained considerable popularity as the decades progressed and was adopted by many makers of both quilts and coverlets.

65. Embroidered Blanket

Maker unknown
New York State or New England, about 1835
Wool and cotton
Rogers Fund, 1941 (41.183)

The patterning on this piece, which was probably made about a decade after our other embroidered blanket (catalogue no. 64), breaks all ties with eighteenth-century design motifs. With its classical medallions embroidered in white cotton thread on an indigo blue wool base, it is obviously a handmade imitation of the popular professionally woven Jacquard coverlets of the day. Although the piece was listed as being from New England on the Museum documents prepared when it entered the collection in 1941, the type of blue and white double cloth coverlet that was the blanket maker's inspiration was more typically found in New York State. (For comparison, see catalogue nos. 52, 53.)

Most coverlet weavers working in the middle decades of the nineteenth century charged between two and three dollars per woven coverlet. The enterprising maker of this embroidered blanket attained the elegant effect of a woven coverlet at a fraction of the cost. The wool for the twill-woven blanket base could have been shorn from the family's own sheep and was most likely carded, spun, dyed, and woven at home. By the early years of the nineteenth century, the cotton thread used to embroider the design in economy and stem stitches was being manufactured in factories up and down the East Coast and could be purchased for a few pennies. The end product is a unique testament to its unknown maker's ingenuity and talent for design.

66. Embroidered Bed Curtain

Sarah Noyes Chester (1722–1797)
Wethersfield, Hartford County, Connecticut, about 1745
Linen and wool
Gift of Mr. and Mrs. Frank Coit Johnson, through their sons and
daughter, 1944 (44.140)

The maker of our embroidered bed curtain, Sarah Noyes Chester, is one of a few eighteenth-century craftswomen whose image is known, through a portrait painted in about 1780 (Figure 13). Additionally, more information exists about her life than about those of most eighteenth-century American women. Sarah was born in 1722, the daughter of the Reverend James Noyes, pastor of the First Church of New Haven, Connecticut. On November 19, 1747, at the age of twenty-five, she married Colonel John Chester (1703–1771) of Wethersfield, who was nineteen years her senior. Sarah's husband died in 1771, while he was inspecting a hayfield. From contemporary accounts of his death, it seems that he suffered a sudden heart attack. According to his obituary, Colonel John Chester was one of the wealthiest men in Wethersfield and held many important posts in the community, including Judge of the County Court. After twenty-six years of widowhood, Sarah died at the age of seventy-five on January 25, 1797. Both she and her husband rest in Wethersfield's Ancient Burying Ground. The couple had six children: four sons and two daughters. Our needlework descended through the family of her third child, a daughter named Sarah, who married Thomas Coit of Norwich, Connecticut.

Although for many years this piece was thought to be a coverlet, recent research has proved that it is actually a curtain from a set of bed hangings. The set was embroidered in about 1745, perhaps in preparation for Sarah Noyes Chester's marriage. Until the nineteenth century, bed hangings were an essential part of the furnishings of any home. A complete set of bed hangings included four curtains suspended from a frame that were drawn around the bed, a stationary curtain hung at the head of the bed called a head cloth, valances that covered the top rail of the frame and hid the top edges of the four curtains, a tester cloth that was stretched over the top of the frame, and often, a matching coverlet. The two movable curtains that hung close to the head of the bed were usually one-half the width of the curtains that hung at the foot. The two narrow head curtains (90 x 37½ inches) and a valance from the set of bed hangings made by Sarah Noyes Chester are in the collection of the Webb-Deane-Stevens Museum in Wethersfield. They are there because Sarah's daughter Abigail married Joseph Webb, Jr., whose father built the house that is now this museum. The composition of the embroidery on our panel matches these pieces, and the size of the panel (87¾ x 70⅝ inches) further indicates that it is one of the wide foot curtains from the same set. Only one of the eighteenth-century wool-embroidered linen "bed coverings" in our collection (catalogue no. 68) was actually a coverlet when it was first created. Most of our other pieces of this type are either bed curtains that have been mistaken for bed coverings in the past or coverlets that were made at a later date by piecing together bed curtains and valances. When completely draped beds went out of style soon after the turn of the nineteenth century, many families still appreciated the work of their mothers or grandmothers, and sets of these beautifully wrought embroidered bed hangings were often transformed into coverlets.

Figure 13. Portrait of Sarah Noyes Chester. Artist unknown, about 1780. Oil on canvas, 30¾ × 25½ in. Courtesy, The Wethersfield Historical Society, Wethersfield, Connecticut

67. Embroidered Coverlet

Mary Breed (1751–?)
Probably New London County, Connecticut, 1770
Linen/cotton and wool
Rogers Fund, 1922 (22.55)

When the panels of this coverlet were embroidered in 1770, they were not meant to be constructed into a bed covering at all. Originally, they were two narrow bed curtains and three bed valances, most likely stitched together in the early nineteenth century. Some of the embroidery has been chopped away at the foot end so that the converted coverlet could accommodate bedposts more easily.

When the coverlet came into the Museum's collection in 1922, it was attributed to Mary Breed, aged nineteen in 1770, who was said to have lived on Breed's Hill, Charlestown (now Boston), Massachusetts. The eighteenth-century inscription embroidered on the piece, which read: *MARY BREED/AGE 19 Y 1770*, is now mostly worn away and can be seen clearly only in old photographs. That the piece was stitched on Breed's Hill, where the 1775 Battle of Bunker Hill actually took place, was particularly appealing to the collectors of the 1920s, who were interested in the historical resonance of all things colonial. However, with further study of American textile arts, it became evident that particular styles of eighteenth-century embroidery could be accurately assigned to specific areas in the American colonies. In her 1973 article on crewel wool-embroidered bed hangings, Anne Pollard Rowe found our Mary Breed coverlet problematic. There are a number of pieces of needlework in other museums' collections in the same embroidery style as Mary Breed's. Called the "symmetrical style" by Rowe, it is characterized by sprays of flowers and trees that are symmetrical in composition. Each spray contains only one type of flower, and birds, often in pairs, are also a prominent feature. Except for one set of valances, all the known pieces of bed hangings in this style can be documented to Connecticut, and two pieces especially close to Mary Breed's coverlet can be further documented to towns in New London County. Since the provenance of our piece was unquestioned, Rowe (pp. 149–50) concluded that although the coverlet was the only one in the symmetrical style documented to Boston, "The mere presence of the symmetrical designs in Boston suggests a Bostonian source [for the entire style], but the exact method by which it may have been dispersed is uncertain." Most Boston embroidered bed hangings of the same period were considerably more formal and closer to English precedents than Mary Breed's coverlet.

After further puzzling over the piece, we decided to try to identify Mary Breed. Because we knew she was nineteen in 1770, it might be possible to track down the birth of a daughter to a Breed family in 1751. At first, we tried the Boston area, but as we had begun to expect, no Mary Breeds were found to be born there at that time. Connecticut proved more fruitful; the records show that a Mary Breed was born on February 9, 1751, to John and Silence Breed of New London. This is the only recorded Mary Breed born in either Massachusetts or Connecticut in 1751, and since our coverlet much more closely resembles pieces from New London County than any from Boston, it is most probable that our work was made in that location. We may never know where the Boston attribution originated, but because there was a Breed family of Boston and all the Breeds in New England at the time could have been related, perhaps a later owner of the piece became confused as to its true origin.

68

68. Embroidered Coverlet

Ruth Culver Coleman
Possibly Sag Harbor, Suffolk County, New York, about 1760–75
Linen and wool
Sansbury-Mills Fund, 1961 (61.48.1)

69. Embroidered Bed Hangings

Ruth Culver Coleman
Possibly Sag Harbor, Suffolk County, New York, about 1760–75
Linen, linen/cotton, and wool
Sansbury-Mills Fund, 1961 (61.48.2)

This magnificent bed cover and set of bed hangings (currently sewn together into a second coverlet) are undoubtedly the finest eighteenth-century American embroideries in our collection. Both a name and a probable location can be assigned to them, but for now, a number of elements in their attribution remain unsure. As far as we know, the pieces were made by Ruth Culver Coleman of Sag Harbor, a small town at the eastern tip of Long Island, New York. Although they resemble work that is regularly attributed to Connecticut, in about 1898, Margaret Whiting of the Deerfield (Massachusetts) Society of Blue and White Needlework took photographs of them while on a visit to Sag Harbor and identified them as the work of one-time resident Ruth Culver Coleman. Whiting was a crusader in the cause of repopularizing eighteenth-century American handicrafts, especially needlework. The location does not seem completely out of line when one remembers that Sag Harbor was an active fishing community during the eighteenth and nineteenth centuries, and since New London was not many miles away, easily accessible across Long Island Sound, there were probably exchanges between the communities at the eastern end of Long Island and those on the Connecticut coast. The pieces could have been made in Connecticut and imported with a bride to Long Island, or it is possible that only the patterns for the embroidery designs traveled across the Sound.

In 1909, one or both of these pieces was displayed at the Metropolitan as part of the exhibition that accompanied the Hudson-Fulton Celebration, which commemorated the three hundredth anniversary of Henry Hudson's discovery of the river that bears his name and the hundredth anniversary of Robert Fulton's first successful voyage up the Hudson in the steamboat *Clermont*. Item 592 in the exhibition's catalogue notes: "Embroidery. Homespun white linen with elaborate design of flowers and leaves embroidered in crewel work. Designs copied from a piece of French printed cotton in the possession of the owner. American, Eighteenth Century. Lent by Miss Mulford." Miss Mulford was the daughter of Ezekiel and Julia Prentice Mulford of Sag Harbor. Ezekiel was the owner and agent of whaling ships. Julia Prentice Mulford's grandfather was Benjamin Coleman (perhaps the husband of Ruth Culver Coleman), who, after moving from Nantucket, was living in Sag Harbor by 1776. As far back as Benjamin, the family probably made their living from shipping or fishing. Although the 1790 Census shows both Colemans and Culvers living in the Sag Harbor area, Ruth Culver Coleman has never been definitively identified. As always, official records of eighteenth- and early nineteenth-century women who were not heads of households are scarce.

Aspects to the objects themselves are also puzzling. Were the designs really copied from a piece of French printed cotton? The reference in the Museum's 1909 catalogue to the fabric in Miss Mulford's possession is enticing in this regard. When were the all-blue wool-embroidered bed hangings (catalogue no. 69) made into a bed cover, and were all of the pieces stitched together from the same set? When Margaret Whiting took her photographs in 1898, the all-blue pieces were already sewn together. The illustration shows that the blue coverlet is made up of many lengths of fabric. Some of these base fabrics are all linen; others have a linen warp and a cotton weft. The two long panels at either side of the piece, which may have been the two head curtains, are the most elaborately embroidered and most closely match the motifs on our coverlet (catalogue no. 68). The three smaller pieces at the coverlet's center have a different base fabric, and the embroidered motifs are less confidently wrought. There are three fragmentary pieces at the top right of the coverlet that are of yet another base fabric of a slightly different weave. Because of the variety of base fabrics, it is questionable whether or not all of the pieces are from the same set of bed hangings. If they are all from one set, did Ruth Culver Coleman embroider them all herself? If one considers the diversity of fabrics and designs, it looks as though a number of different hands may have been involved.

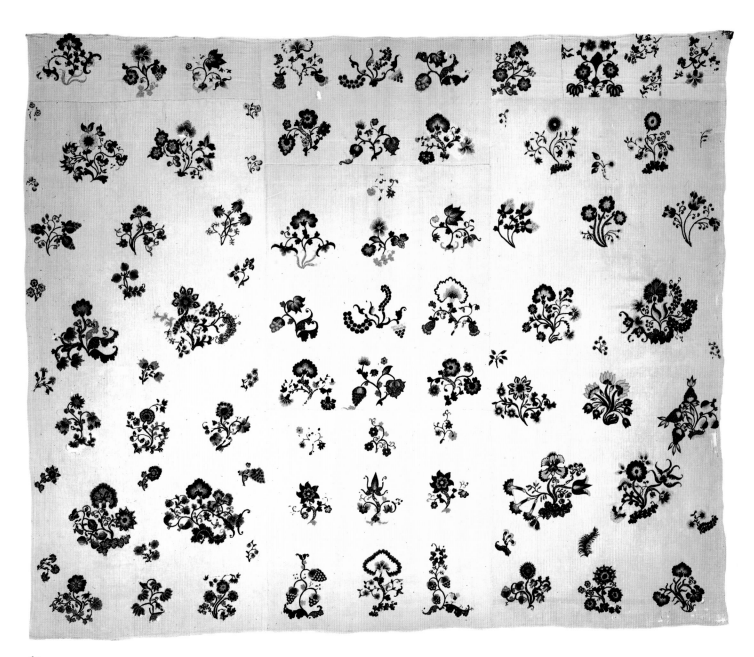

69

70. Embroidered Whitework Coverlet

Mary Walker Stith Jones (1802–1884)
Breckinridge County, Kentucky, about 1815–18
Cotton
Fletcher Fund, 1939 (39.111)

Whitework bed covers in all techniques—stuffed (see catalogue no. 43), embroidered, and tufted—were popular throughout the United States during the first decades of the nineteenth century. This embroidered coverlet is one of a number of similar whitework pieces with drawnwork panels that hail from Kentucky. The all-cotton coverlet is particularly interesting because it is actually a large-scale sampler of needlework techniques.

The coverlet's maker is Mary Walker Stith Jones, born June 10, 1802, in Bedford County, Virginia, the oldest child of Benjamin and Phoebe Cocke Stith. The family moved to Breckinridge County, Kentucky, when she was still a small child. The only formal schooling she received was one session at a Catholic school in Bethlehem, Henry County, Kentucky, where, among other skills, she was taught needlework. At not quite fifteen years of age, on March 27, 1817, she married her cousin William Bolling Jones. They had twelve children altogether, the first born in about 1818, and the last born in May of 1844, when Mary Stith Jones was almost forty-two. In 1865, the family moved to Nodaway County, Missouri. She died on December 20, 1884, at the home of her youngest son, in Fayetteville, Arkansas, and was buried in Miriam Cemetery, Maryville, Nodaway County, Missouri. Our coverlet descended to her granddaughter Bertie, the daughter of her youngest son.

According to her descendants, Mary Stith Jones began the coverlet in 1815 when she was thirteen years old and completed it in 1818 when she was already a married woman, signing it with a delicate *J* for Jones in the lower left corner. The cotton base fabric on which she embroidered was supposedly woven at the Stith family farm. Her father, Benjamin, owned slaves, and among them was a man named Morley, who was an expert weaver. The Stith's farm grew cotton and flax, and according to family history, the cotton for the cloth, thread, and fringe was grown at home, where Morley wove the cotton into cloth for her to embroider with homespun thread.

71. Embroidered Coverlet and Pillow Sham

A. P. Lalkers (?)
United States, 1898
Linen, cotton, and silk
Purchase, Mrs. Roger Brunschwig Gift, 1986 (1986.333.1,2)

A number of diverse factors helped bring about the art needlework movement that arose in late nineteenth-century America. With the beginning of women's suffrage came women's realization that financial independence was as important as political freedom. Since, as a rule, they were not trained to go into business of any type, needlework and similar handicrafts were most women's only resource. Organizations such as the New York Women's Exchange were created to sell the products from a woman's hand on the open market and to allow them to make a living independently of their husbands or fathers for the first time. Concurrently—perhaps in an effort to appease women who, still firmly rooted to their homes, were beginning to acknowledge their frustration with their powerless state—a philosophy flourished that both confirmed a woman's place in her home and suggested that she could gain power in the world by bettering the lives of her husband and children through her artistic decoration of their home. It was believed that the culture and tranquillity she fostered in the home through this type of decoration would in turn refine her family and motivate them to venture out and make a finer world. The opening of Japan to the West and the ensuing influx of beautifully designed and ornamented Japanese objects into America, as well as the 1876 Centennial, which focused Americans on the rediscovery of their colonial roots, also contributed to the reawakening of many craftswomen's creative interests.

The decorators and designers of this period rebelled against the coarse and harshly colored Berlin woolwork and cross-stitch needlework that abounded at mid-century. They encouraged women to rediscover natural dyes and to produce stitchery based on earlier models. In the well-known volume titled *Art Embroidery, A Treatise on the Revived Practice of Decorative Needlework*, published in London in 1878 by M. S. Lockwood and E. Glaister (pp. 70–71), the authors suggested:

> Better models may be found in the freer work of the 17th and 18th centuries, and the early part of the present century. All embroidery on linen grounds, whether in silks or worsteds, is well worthy of attention. In this style are the massive quilts of the 17th century, with bold flower patterns overlaying an elaborately quilted ground, all done in silk. . . . There is also coarser work of the same century in crewel worsteds; some of these are very handsome and well designed. . . . We can hardly study the needlework of the 18th century too much. . . . It is because the work of this time is thoughtful and original that it is worthy of our earnest attention.

By the late nineteenth century, many women were sewing for pleasure rather than purely out of necessity, and a number of needlework companies were formed in response to their desire for more creative possibilities. Our 1898 coverlet and pillow sham are embroidered in silks following a pattern stamped

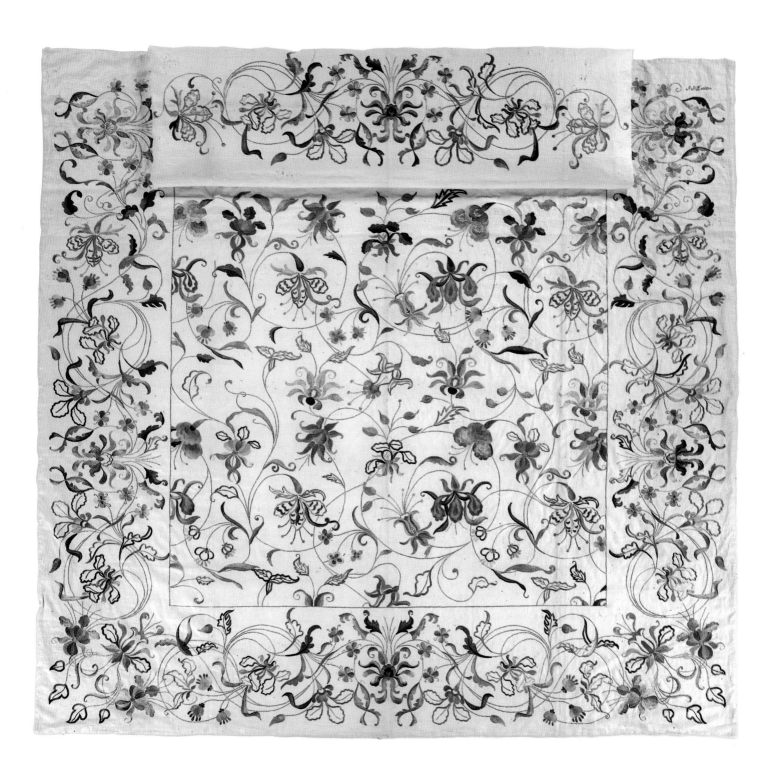

in blue on the linen base. Many companies offered a wide variety of prestamped objects—mats, table scarves, throws, and coverlets—patterned primarily with seminaturalistic flowers. The Brainerd & Armstrong Company of New London, Connecticut, for example, published a pattern book in 1899 titled *Embroidery Lessons*, which gave women instruction on embroidery techniques and offered them a chance to purchase stamped goods for all the projects illustrated in the book. Although Brainerd & Armstrong's wares were available in stores throughout the United States and Canada, the catalogue gave women who lived outside of urban centers access to artistic goods. In their book, the company listed coverlet kits that produced goods that probably were quite similar to our piece:

> Bedspreads of our Silk-Faced Counterpanes.
>
> The stamping is done on Cream Colored, Silk Faced Counterpane goods, made in our own mills. There is nothing more elegant than one of these spreads after the embroidery is completed. They make splendid wedding gifts. Design No. 200 consists of Fleur de Lis (or Iris) stamped on a spread 82 x 90 inches in size. Prices are: Stamped Spread, $12.50; Commenced Spread, $20.00; Finished Spread, $35.00.

Although our coverlet is not a completely original work of art, it yields interesting information about the popular trends and designs of the later years of the nineteenth century. The colors of the silks used to embroider this piece, for instance, resemble the colors of the naturally dyed wools used by Ruth Culver Coleman when she embroidered her coverlet (catalogue no. 68) nearly 125 years earlier. The iris design shows the influence of Japanese art in both subject matter and form, while the curving whiplash lines of the border design owe their conception to the Art Nouveau style that was blossoming on the European continent. Although A. P. Lalkers, the coverlet's embroiderer, did not design the pattern herself, she had good reason to be proud of the painstaking job she had completed so beautifully.

Detail of catalogue no. 71

Catalogue of the Collection

NOTE TO THE READER: The following is a complete catalogue of the 119 American quilts and coverlets in the collection of The Metropolitan Museum of Art. The works are arranged in seven sections according to types. Within each section, they are in chronological order by accession number. An accession number is assigned to every work of art that is a permanent part of the Museum's collection. The first part of this number indicates the year in which the item was acquired. For objects acquired between 1870 and 1969, the year is noted by its last two digits; from 1970 on, all four digits are used. The catalogue number appears for each of the seventy-one pieces featured in the front section of the book. Complete inscriptions, pertinent references, and publications of specific works are also included.

23.80.75   (catalogue no. 3)

Quilt, Hexagon or Honeycomb pattern

Elizabeth Van Horne Clarkson (1771–1852)
New York City, about 1830
107⅝ × 98¼ in.
Top: cotton; *back*: cotton; *binding*: self-bound, edges turned
    into each other and stitched together
Gift of Mr. and Mrs. William A. Moore, 1923

The quilt top is constructed of multicolored hexagons, each
measuring one inch per side. The hexagons are sewn
together with whipstitching. The central medallion and the
border are predominantly brown. The piece is quilted
overall in a diamond grid, except for the border, which is
quilted to follow the stripes printed on the fabric.

Publications: Bordes 1974, no. 3; Finley 1929, pl. 15; Ickis
1959, pp. 130–32.
References: Colby 1958; Gunn 1988; Rae 1987.

46.152.2

Quilt, Star of Bethlehem pattern

Members of the congregation of the First Baptist Church
Perth Amboy, Middlesex County, New Jersey, about 1845–48
76¼ × 75⅞ in.
Top: cotton; *back*: cotton; *binding*: self-bound, front turned
    over back and stitched
Gift of Mrs. George Sands Bryan, in memory of her husband,
    George Sands Bryan, 1946

The central Star of Bethlehem is pieced of multicolored
printed cottons and edged with a red and white cotton
sawtooth border. It is surrounded by blocks appliquéd with
brown plaid oak leaf forms. The piece is quilted in a variety
of simple patterns.

Notes: This quilt was given to the Museum by the granddaughter-in-law of the Reverend George Faitute Hendrickson
(1817–1894). Reverend Hendrickson was a Baptist minister
for more than fifty years. Between the years 1845 and 1848,
he was pastor of the First Baptist Church, which at the time
stood on the northwest corner of High and Fayette streets
in Perth Amboy. According to his granddaughter-in-law, the
quilt was made by members of his congregation and given
to him, along with fruits and vegetables, during a Harvest
Festival.

Back of 47.39   (catalogue no. 24)

Quilt, Hexagon or Mosaic pattern

Anne Record
New Bedford, Bristol County, Massachusetts, begun in 1864
87 × 75½ in.
Top: silk and silk velvet; *back*: silk; *binding*: narrow ends
    finished with silk cording
Gift of Mrs. Frederick H. Buzzee, 1947

This pieced bed cover has a top composed of hexagons of
multicolored silks, including cut velvets, plaids, prints, and
brocades. Each colored rosette (made from seven hexagons)
is set off by six surrounding hexagons of plain black silk.
The bed cover is unquilted; the batting is attached to the
top with an inner layer of brown printed-silk chiffon
through which long zigzag running stitches are sewn. The
sides are turned under and sewn together. Large silk rectangles are pieced together to form the back.

References: Colby 1958; Gunn 1988; Rae 1987.

48.134.1

Quilt, Star of Bethlehem pattern variation

Maker unknown
United States, about 1840–50
112½ × 107 in.
Top: cotton; *back*: cotton; *binding*: self-bound, back turned
over front and stitched
Gift of Mr. and Mrs. Sidney Hosmer, 1948

The top is pieced of a variety of printed cottons set on a
white ground. There is diamond quilting in the white areas,
while in the pieced areas, lines of stitching, spaced one-half
inch apart, follow the stars' outlines. There are nine Stars of
Bethlehem, each pieced of various red and brown fabrics.
The border is of a brown-ground glazed chintz, and the
backing is of plain white woven cotton.

Notes: The quilt descended through the family of
Mr. Sidney Hosmer, one of the donors, but no precise
history was gathered when it was accessioned. Some fabrics
in this quilt are the same as those in quilt 48.134.2.

48.134.2

Quilt, Flying Geese pattern

Maker unknown
United States, about 1840–50
112¼ × 114⅝ in.
Top: cotton; *back*: cotton; *binding*: cotton tape
Gift of Mr. and Mrs. Sidney Hosmer, 1948

The top has pieced rows alternating with bands of chintz.
The pieced rows are quilted in chevrons, while the chintz
rows are diamond quilted. The border is quilted with diagonal parallel lines. The Flying Geese triangles are cut from a
variety of small cotton prints, primarily in shades of browns
and reds. The light brown chintz used for the bands and
border is printed with rose vines. The quilt has a plain
white woven cotton backing and a tape binding striped
in white, brown, blue, and green.

Notes: The quilt descended through the family of Mr.
Sidney Hosmer, one of the donors, but no precise history
was gathered when the piece was accessioned. The floral
chintz stripes appear to be cut from a roller-printed English
fabric of about 1830–40. Some of the triangular patches are
American fabrics from the mid-nineteenth century. The
quilt is in generally poor condition due to significant fading.
Some of the fabrics found in this quilt are the same as those
in quilt 48.134.1.

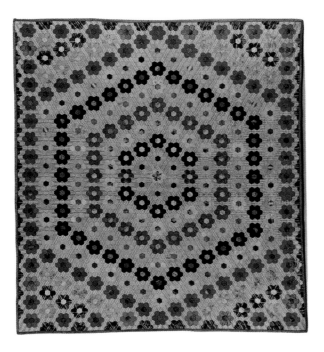

53.58.1 (catalogue no. 25)

Quilt (or decorative throw), Hexagon or Mosaic pattern

Possibly Caroline Brooks Gould
United States, about 1870
55 × 49⅛ in.
Top: silk; *back*: silk; *binding*: silk ribbon
Bequest of Carolyn Fiske MacGregor, in memory of her
    grandmother, Caroline Brooks Gould, 1952

Pieced of one-inch-per-side silk hexagons, this quilt is
completely hand stitched. The striped, changeable silk
backing is attached to the batting with diamond quilting.
The quilt is bound with a silk brocade ribbon, which is
finished in a bow at one corner of the quilt's back. The small
individual hexagons are grouped to form concentric radiat-
ing hexagonal forms.

References: Colby 1958; Gunn 1988; Rae 1987.

Notes: The silks pieced into this quilt can be dated to the
second half of the nineteenth century. The small size of
this quilt indicates that it is from the third quarter of the
nineteenth century, when silk and velvet throws, meant
to be draped over furniture, came into fashion for home
decorating.

62.143

Quilt, Crazy pattern

Aletta Whitehouse Davis (1830?–1925)
New England, about 1885
74¾ × 73½ in.
Top: silk and silk velvet with cotton and chenille embroi-
    dery; *back*: cotton; *binding*: silk-velvet border
Gift of Reverend and Mrs. Karl Nielsen, 1962

Each block of this quilt was pieced and appliquéd onto a
backing, and then embroidered and decorated with a variety of motifs. The blocks are joined together without any
sashing. The joined blocks are surrounded by a five-inch-
wide gold silk-velvet border. The quilt is pieced of many
different colored fabrics, but most blocks feature a larger
patch of black velvet embroidered with a flower. The backing is a brown weft-faced cotton. The piece is not quilted;
the layers are tied together every four inches with blue and
yellow cotton embroidery threads.

Publication: Bordes 1974, no. 9.
Reference: McMorris 1984.

Notes: The maker, Aletta Whitehouse Davis, was the great-
aunt of one of the donors, Reverend Karl Nielsen. According to family history, she was the wife of a ship's captain.
The fabrics and motifs found in this Crazy quilt are quite
common to many Crazy quilts and may indicate that it was
made from a kit.

62.144

Quilt, Star of Bethlehem pattern variation

"Aunt Ellen" and "Aunt Margaret," slaves of the Marmaduke
    Beckwith Morton family
"The Knob," near Russellville, Logan County, Kentucky,
    about 1837–50
88¼ × 87⅛ in.
Top: silk; *back*: cotton; *binding*: silk
Gift of Roger Morton and Dr. Paul C. Morton, 1962

Multicolored and patterned silks make up the very finely
pieced star blocks. These alternate with unpieced
blocks of a pink-and-green changeable silk. The unpieced
blocks have been intricately quilted and stuffed, each
with a different plant or flower. Carded cotton was used for
the stuffed areas and the batting. The edge of the quilt is
bound with lavender silk, and the backing is of solid pink
glazed cotton.

Notes: The history of this quilt was told to donor Roger
Morton by his uncle. Roger Morton quoted his uncle's
remembrances in a letter he wrote to the Museum when he
donated the quilt: "The actual work was done by two slave
women who were skilled seamstresses and were considered
a cut above the other help about the place who did the more
menial work. These women, Aunt Ellen and Aunt Margaret, as we were taught to call them, remained with the
family after emancipation and died at 'The Knob.' As near
as I can determine the quilt was made between the years
1837–1850." The quilt is in very fragile condition due to the
disintegration of the weighted silk top.

62.145   (catalogue no. 13)

Quilt, Double X pattern

Maker unknown
Probably Lancaster, Fairfield County, Ohio, 1849
81⅛ × 84¾ in.
Top: cotton; *back*: cotton; *binding*: cotton
Inscribed (quilted at bottom right corner): *R M/1849*
Gift of Mrs. Emanuel Altman, 1962

Pieced blocks of blue calico and white cotton fabric alternate
with plain white woven cotton blocks on the quilt's top. The
area within the first border is square quilted, and the area
between first and second borders is quilted with a feather
vine that terminates with feather wreaths at each of the four
corners. There are two blue and white zigzag borders. The
binding and backing are of plain white woven cotton.

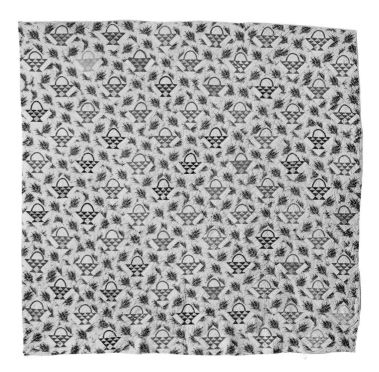

1971.180.125   (catalogue no. 39)

Quilt, Strip pattern

Maker unknown
United States or England, about 1825
102¼ × 89¼ in.
Top: cotton; *back*: cotton; *binding*: self-bound, edges turned
    into each other and stitched together
Bequest of Flora E. Whiting, 1971

This quilt's top is composed of thirteen long strips of six
different English block- and roller-printed fabrics stitched
together in a symmetrical arrangement from the center
strip. It is quilted overall in double-diamond pattern except
for the double swag quilting in the border. The corners were
notched at bottom, probably after the piece was completed.
The backing is of a coarsely woven white cotton, and the
batting is of carded cotton.

1971.180.128

Quilt, Basket pattern

Maker unknown
United States, about 1880–1900
89½ × 89 in.
Top: cotton; *back*: cotton; *binding*: self-bound, back turned
    over front and stitched
Bequest of Flora E. Whiting, 1971

The baskets in the diamond set-blocks are pieced from a
variety of cotton calicos. The blocks are stitched together in
a diagonal grid separated by sashing of beige cotton chintz.
There is diamond quilting in the chintz areas, and quilting
follows the basket design in the pieced blocks. The backing is of plain white woven cotton.

Notes: Some of the fabrics pieced into the basket blocks are
late-nineteenth-century novelty shirting cottons. These
include one with tiny dogs printed in red on a white
ground, and another, printed in purple, of a man shooting
at a bird. The cotton chintz sashing is printed with small-
scale bunches of lilies of the valley.

1973.22 (catalogue no. 28)

Quilt, Log Cabin pattern, Pineapple or Windmill Blades variation

Maker unknown, probably Amish or Mennonite
Pennsylvania, about 1900–1930
89½ × 89¾ in.
Top: cotton; *back*: cotton; *binding*: self-bound, front turned over back and stitched
Purchase, Mr. and Mrs. George M. Kaufman Gift, 1973

The quilt is composed of pieced blocks with patches of solid brown, pumpkin gold, red, and pine-green cotton. Each piece is quilted individually around the edge. The medium brown border is quilted with feather vines and diagonal lines. All the quilting is hand stitched with brown thread. The quilt is backed with a small-scale brown floral-printed cotton.

Publication: Bordes 1974, no. 10.

1973.64 (catalogue no. 8)

Quilt, Star of Bethlehem pattern variation

Maker unknown
Possibly New York State, about 1845
90 × 89¼ in.
Top: cotton; *back*: cotton; *binding*: cotton
Purchase, Mr. and Mrs. Samuel S. Schwartz Gift, 1973

The pieced Stars of Bethlehem appear in three blocks of different sizes. The mid-sized blocks are made into a border. The large central star is surrounded by four smaller stars at the corners. The entire piece is quilted in parallel lines following the outlines of the stars. All of the stars have red centers and concentric rings of diamond-shaped pieces in beige, brown, and light blue printed cottons. The sashing is of a brown printed cotton with colors that are complementary to the colors in the stars. The backing is of plain white woven cotton, and the edge binding is made from the sashing fabric.

Publication: Bordes 1974, no. 5.

1973.94   (catalogue no. 27)

Quilt, Sunshine and Shadow pattern

Maker unknown, Amish
Probably Lancaster County, Pennsylvania, about 1920–40
81 × 76½ in.
Top: wool; *back*: cotton; *binding*: cotton
Purchase, Eva Gebhard-Gourgaud Foundation Gift, 1973

Small wool squares in strong solid colors have been pieced
together to form a quilt top patterned with alternating light
and dark concentric diamond-shaped rings. The wide purple wool border terminates in square navy-blue corner
blocks. Each small square is quilted with an X. The border is
quilted with feather vines. The backing is of brown and
maroon checked cotton. The edge binding is of black cotton.

Publication: Bordes 1974, no. 11.

1973.124   (catalogue no. 29)

Quilt, Squares and Bars pattern

Maker unknown, Amish
Probably Lancaster County, Pennsylvania, 1892
84¾ × 78⅛ in.
Top: wool; *back*: wool; *binding*: wool
Inscribed (embroidered at bottom center of central patch):
    18 A K 92
Gift of Mr. and Mrs. Stanley Tananbaum, 1973

The top of this quilt has large squares and bars in solid
green, rust, purple, and maroon wool with a blue-green
binding. The backing is of navy-blue wool. All the fabrics,
except for the backing, seem home dyed. The quilt was
pieced and bound on a sewing machine. The quilting is
hand stitched; the center square and narrow sidebars
are diamond quilted, the corner blocks are quilted with
baskets of fruit, and the border is quilted with tulips and
fiddlehead ferns.

Publication: Bishop 1975, p. 57.

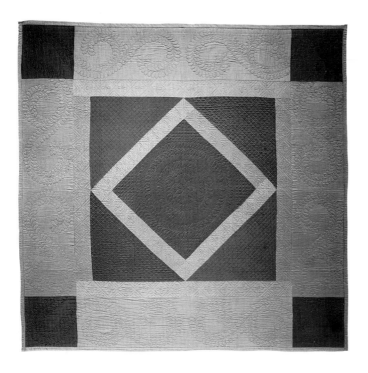

1973.157   (catalogue no. 26)

Quilt, Center Diamond pattern

Maker unknown, Amish
Lancaster County, Pennsylvania, about 1910–40
79 × 79¼ in.
Top: wool and cotton; *back*: cotton; *binding*: cotton
Sansbury-Mills Fund, 1973

The top of this quilt is pieced of dark green, dark red, and
cadet-blue wool. The backing is a navy-blue cotton shot
through at random with colored threads. All the stitching,
aside from the quilting, was done on a sewing machine.
The center diamond is quilted with a seven-pointed star,
which is enclosed by two feather wreaths. The narrow red
inner borders are quilted with pumpkin-seed flowers, while
the wide outer border is feather quilted.

1973.158

Quilt, Log Cabin pattern, Barn Raising variation

Maker unknown
Possibly Pennsylvania, about 1890–1910
84⅜ × 80¾ in.
Top: cotton and wool; *back*: cotton; *binding*: cotton
Purchase, Eva Gebhard-Gourgaud Foundation Gift, 1973

Pieced blocks of multicolored printed cotton fabrics are
joined together in this quilt's top. There is a beige floral-
print border. The back is composed of alternating strips of
the border fabric and another cotton with a small-scale
print. The binding is made of solid red woven cotton. The
piece is fan quilted overall.

1973.159   (catalogue no. 20)

Quilt, Log Cabin pattern, Light and Dark variation

Maker unknown
Possibly Pennsylvania, about 1865
92½ × 80 in.
Top: wool and cotton; *back*: cotton; *binding*: wool
Purchase, Eva Gebhard-Gourgaud Foundation Gift, 1973

The quilt's top is composed of pieced blocks of multicolored
and patterned wools and cottons, each block with a center
of red wool challis. The border is pieced of the same fabrics
as the blocks. The back is of printed cotton. There is
quilting along the edges of each small piece of fabric. There
is no batting between the front and back layers.

1973.160

Quilt, Bars pattern

Maker unknown, Amish
Probably Lancaster County, Pennsylvania,
    about 1900–1950
75 × 71¾ in.
Top: cotton; *back*: cotton; *binding*: cotton
Purchase, Eva Gebhard-Gourgaud Foundation Gift, 1973

The quilt top is pieced of what appear to be hand-dyed
fabrics in shades of gray-green, gray-blue, and deep red.
The backing is a blue warp, white weft cotton. All the
stitching, except the quilting, is done by sewing machine.
The piece is somewhat crudely quilted. The center bars are
diamond quilted, the inner border is quilted with a flower
vine, and the outer border is rope quilted.

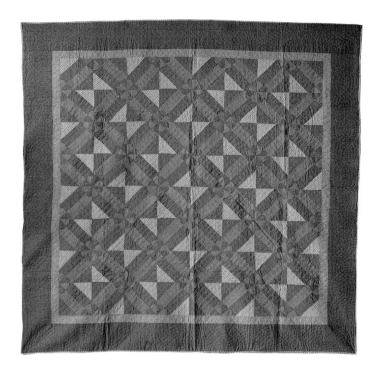

1973.161

Quilt, Hearts and Gizzards pattern variation

Maker unknown
Pennsylvania, about 1930–50
86¾ × 84¾ in.
Top: cotton; *back*: cotton; *binding*: cotton
Purchase, Paul P. Ramos Gift, 1973

The quilt top is pieced of cotton calicos: two different pink fabrics, two different yellow fabrics, and one blue fabric. The backing has a beige background floral print of definite twentieth-century character. The binding is yellow calico. The bed cover is quilted overall in a diamond pattern, except for the outer pink border, which is rope quilted. Aside from the quilting, the piece is almost entirely machine stitched.

Reference: Lasansky 1985.

1973.204   (catalogue no. 7)

Quilt, Star of Bethlehem pattern

Maker unknown
Possibly Maryland, about 1835
122 × 122 in.
Top: cotton; *back*: cotton; *binding*: self-bound, back turned over front and stitched
Sansbury-Mills Fund, 1973

Multicolored printed cotton fabrics make up the large star at the center of this pieced and appliquéd quilt. The border, as well as the flower and bird appliqués, is of a high quality English chintz. The appliqués are embroidered around their edges with buttonhole stitch. The pieced central star is unquilted, and the white woven cotton areas are diamond quilted with ten-pointed stuffed stars appearing at intervals.

Publication: Bordes 1974, no. 4.
References: Allen 1987; "Little-Known Masterpieces II" 1922; Montgomery 1970, fig. 380.

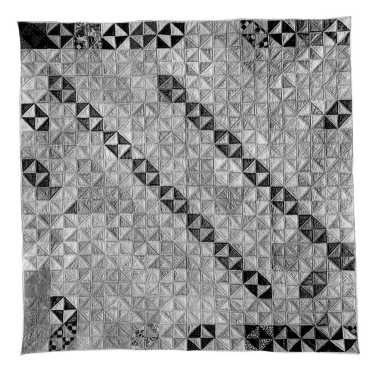

1973.205   (catalogue no. 23)

Quilt, Broken Dishes pattern

Maker unknown
Possibly Ohio, about 1920
77 × 76½ in.
Top: silk; *back*: cotton; *binding*: cotton
Sansbury-Mills Fund, 1973

This quilt is pieced of silks, predominantly in solid shades of yellow, orange, and pink. A few pieces of printed fabric appear toward the outer edge of the quilt. The backing and binding are of a solid yellow cotton. Each triangular piece is outline quilted about one-quarter inch from its edge.

Publication: Bordes 1974, no. 12.

1974.32   (catalogue no. 15)

Quilt, Eagle pattern

Maker unknown
Possibly New England, about 1837–50
103 × 97 in.
Top: cotton; *back*: cotton; *binding*: self-bound, back turned
    over front and stitched
Gift of Mrs. Jacob M. Kaplan, 1974

The central area of this quilt's top is appliquéd with a large eagle of brown calico, topped by twenty-six dark blue calico six-pointed stars. The shield on the eagle's chest is made of appliquéd red cotton fabric stripes on a light blue fabric. The foliage beneath the eagle is of a brown and blue print. The central area is surrounded by four pieced borders. From the center outward, they are a sawtooth border of red and white, a wider sawtooth of pink and white, a zigzag of medium blue and white, and a sawtooth of red and white. Quilted parallel lines follow the border patterns, while the central area is quilted with hearts and stars. The backing is of plain white woven cotton.

Publication: Safford and Bishop 1972, pp. 154–55.

1974.34   (catalogue no. 31)

Quilt, Crazy pattern

Maker unknown, probably Quaker
Pennsylvania, about 1885–1900
75¾ × 73⅜ in.
Top: silk, silk velvet; *back*: wool; *binding*: self-bound, front
   turned over back and stitched
Purchase, Virginia Groomes Gift, in memory of Mary W.
   Groomes, 1974

The front of this quilt is composed of diamond-set pieced
Crazy blocks alternating with solid beige silk blocks. The
Crazy blocks are hand pieced of silks and silk velvets in
subdued shades of red, gray, brown, mauve, and beige.
While a sewing machine was used for joining the blocks and
attaching the binding, all the quilting is hand stitched with
red cotton thread. The central area is surrounded by an
inner sawtooth border with quilted hearts in each "tooth."
The outer border is both diamond and feather quilted. The
plain silk blocks are quilted with feather wreaths. The
backing is of red wool.

Publications: Bordes 1974, no. 8; Orlofsky 1974, pl. 82.
References: Herr 1985; Herr 1988.

1974.37   (catalogue no. 19)

Quilt, Log Cabin pattern, Straight Furrow
   variation

Maker unknown
United States, about 1865
87½ × 88½ in.
Top: wool; *back*: cotton; *binding*: wool
Purchase, Eva Gebhard-Gourgaud Foundation Gift and
   funds from various donors, 1974

The top of this Log Cabin quilt is pieced of a number of
different printed wool challises. Many of the fabrics have
shades of purple in their designs. The center (or hearth) of
each block is a piece of solid bright magenta challis. The
border is pieced of alternating dark and light challis. Each
small piece of fabric is quilted around its edge. The quilt is
backed with a brown and red printed cotton.

Publication: Bordes 1974, no. 7.

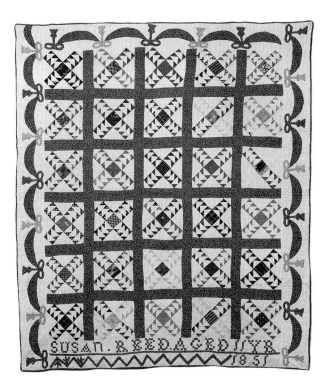

1974.154 (catalogue no. 21)

Quilt, Star of Lemoyne pattern variation

Maker unknown
United States, about 1860
85 × 70 in.
Top: silk; *back*: cotton; *binding*: silk
Gift of Mrs. Gilbert Chapman, 1974

The ground fabric of this quilt top is black silk. The stars are pieced of a variety of colored silks. The plain black blocks are diamond quilted. Each individual piece of silk that combines to form the stars is quilted around its edges. The quilt's backing is of a dull green glazed cotton, and the binding is of red silk.

1976.198.1 (catalogue no. 10)

Quilt, Wild Goose Chase pattern

Susan Reed Ruddick (1839–1869)
Forestburgh, Sullivan County, New York, 1851
86¼ × 73 in.
Top: cotton; *back*: cotton; *binding*: cotton
Inscribed (appliquéd in small squares across bottom edge):
    SUSAN. REED. AGED 11 YR/1851
Gift of Mrs. William Rhinelander Stewart, 1976

This quilt's top is composed of pieced blocks of multi-colored calicos, stitched together with sashing of green calico. The border is appliquéd with green and beige calico swags. The edge binding is of a different green cotton fabric from that used in the sashing. The backing is of plain white woven cotton. The quilting follows the outline of the swags and the crossed Wild Goose Chase designs, while the plain white areas between the crosses and around the border are quilted with hearts.

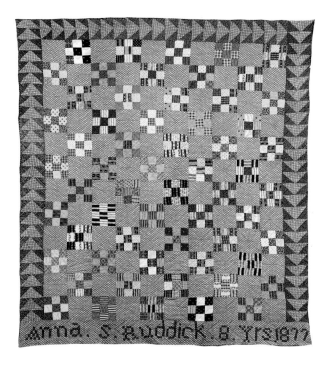

1976.198.2   (catalogue no. 11)

Crib Quilt, Log Cabin pattern, Light and Dark variation

Probably Anna Susan Ruddick Trowbridge (1869–1949)
Monticello, Sullivan County, New York, about 1875
33¾ × 27½ in.
Top: cotton and wool; *back*: cotton; *binding*: self-bound, back turned over front and stitched
Gift of Mrs. William Rhinelander Stewart, 1976

The quilt's top is pieced of cotton and wool, primarily in shades of brown. The light colored patches are of small print cotton shirting fabric. The centers of the "log cabins" are rust-colored wool. The backing is of a brown and red printed cotton fabric. The piece is completely hand stitched and is unquilted.

1976.198.3   (catalogue no. 12)

Quilt, Nine Patch pattern

Anna Susan Ruddick Trowbridge (1869–1949)
Monticello, Sullivan County, New York, 1877
83¼ × 73¼ in.
Top: cotton; *back*: cotton; *binding*: self-bound, back turned over front and stitched
Inscribed (appliquéd in small squares at bottom): *Anna. S. Ruddick. 8. Yrs. 1877*
Gift of Mrs. William Rhinelander Stewart, 1976

This quilt's top is pieced of calicos, primarily in shades of browns and rusts. The backing fabric is a dark brown calico. The inscription is appliquéd on the bottom edge. It is quilted in a variety of patterns; each small square in the Nine Patch blocks is quilted with an *X*. The Flying Geese border is chevron quilted.

1979.22

Quilt (or decorative throw), Roman Stripes pattern

Julia Perry Brigham (1830?–1871)
Wyoming County, New York, about 1865
61 × 52½ in.
Top: silk and silk velvet; *back*: cotton; *binding*: silk velvet
Gift of Katharine Brigham, 1979

The quilt top is pieced in narrow strips of patterned and plain silks and silk velvets in shades of purple, navy-blue, black, maroon, and brown. There are some lighter-colored silks in the horizontal strips. The back is of a faded pink cotton fabric, and the binding is of black velvet. The piece is unquilted; the layers are tied together at wide intervals with pink cotton thread.

Notes: The small size of this piece seems to indicate that it was used as a decorative textile draped over a chair, table, or sofa. Throws such as this one were very much in style during the last decades of the nineteenth century.

1980.498.1   (catalogue no. 4)

Quilt, Hexagon or Honeycomb pattern

Rebecca Davis
United States, 1846
95 × 85⅜ in.
Top: cotton; *back*: cotton; *binding*: self-bound, back turned over front and stitched
Inscribed (in ink at center of a lower righthand rosette):
    Rebecca Davis/1846/March
Gift of Mrs. Andrew Galbraith Carey, 1980

The top of this pieced quilt is composed of hexagons of multicolored and patterned fabrics typical of the 1840s, including some rainbow prints. The hexagons are about two inches per side, except for a small six-pointed star at the center, which is made up of one-half inch-per-side hexagons. There is quilting in parallel diagonal lines in the printed fabric hexagons and in various flower and star forms in the white cotton hexagons. The quilt has a plain white woven cotton back and cotton batting.

Notes: This quilt is the only one of a group of three quilts (1980.498.1–3; see p. 204) that is signed, but all three are assumed to have been made by Rebecca Davis. Most of the printed fabrics are probably of English manufacture. The other two quilts in this group have several fabrics that show English registry marks. All three quilts employ pieces of the same fabrics.

1980.498.2　(catalogue no. 5)

Quilt, Nine Patch pattern variation

Rebecca Davis
United States, about 1846
84¾ × 82¾ in.
Top: cotton; *back*: cotton; *binding*: self-bound, back turned
　over front and stitched
Gift of Mrs. Andrew Galbraith Carey, 1980

This pieced quilt is patterned with Nine Patch blocks within
a diamond-shaped grid. The sashing is of red calico, and
the blocks are pieced from various multicolored and patterned fabrics. The back is of plain white woven cotton, and
the quilt is filled with cotton batting. Except for feather
quilting in the inner white border, the piece is diamond
quilted overall. There are partial English design registration
marks on some pieces of fabric.

1980.498.3　(catalogue no. 6)

Quilt, Star of Lemoyne pattern

Rebecca Davis
United States, about 1846
94 × 80 in.
Top: cotton; *back*: cotton; *binding*: self-bound, back turned
　over front and stitched
Gift of Mrs. Andrew Galbraith Carey, 1980

The eight-pointed stars that decorate this quilt's top are
pieced of multicolored and patterned fabrics typical of the
1840s, including some rainbow prints. In the pieced blocks,
the quilting stitches follow the star shapes with parallel
lines. In the plain white blocks, the quilting pattern alternates between four tulips and four leaves. The quilt has a
cotton-batting filling, and the back is of plain white woven
cotton. There are partial English design registration marks
on some pieces of fabric.

Notes: An almost complete English design registration
mark on a piece of the lavender fabric in this quilt dates that
fabric to 1844.

1983.349   (catalogue no. 34)

Quilt (or decorative throw), Crazy pattern

Tamar Horton Harris North (1833–1905)
North's Landing, Indiana, about 1877
54½ × 55 in.
Top: silk and silk velvet, cotton and cotton lace; *back*: silk;
  binding: self-bound, edges turned into each other and
  stitched together
Inscribed (in purple ink): *Grace Gertrude North./Born
  March 24, 1856/Died Feb. 13 1877.*
Gift of Mr. and Mrs. John S. Cooper, 1983

The top of this quilt is composed of nine pieced blocks
surrounded by a black plaid silk border with corner blocks
of black moiré. The backing is of a maroon satin filled with
cotton and machine quilted in a shell pattern. The top is
stitched to the backing at wide intervals. The Crazy patches
and border are embroidered with both cotton thread and
chenille. Some patches are decorated with paint as well as
embroidery.

Publications: Burke et al. 1986, p. 103; Rodriguez Roque
1984, pp. 90–91.

1988.24.1   (catalogue no. 35)

Quilt, Fan pattern

Maker unknown
United States, about 1900
76½ × 75¾ in.
Top: cotton; *back*: cotton; *binding*: cotton
Purchase, Mrs. Roger Brunschwig Gift, 1988

The blocks of this quilt display pieced fan shapes of solid
red cotton. The ground fabric is of a white cotton printed
with tiny blue polka dots. The backing is of plain white
woven cotton, and the edge binding is of commercially
woven bias tape. The quilting follows the fan shapes in each
block. The quilt is hand stitched, except for the binding,
which is stitched on by sewing machine.

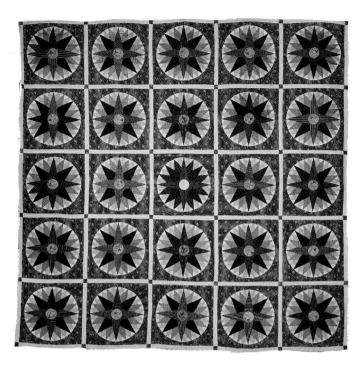

L.1988.55   (catalogue no. 9)

Quilt, Mariner's Compass pattern

Barbara Ann Miller
Pennsylvania, 1847
108 × 107½ in.
Top: cotton and linen; *back*: cotton; *binding*: self-bound,
   back turned over front and stitched
Inscribed (in ink at center of central block):
   Barbara Ann Miller/her quilt/1847
Promised Gift of The Hascoe Foundation

The quilt's top is composed of twenty-five pieced blocks
within a five-block by five-block grid. Each block is bordered by white linen sashing. Many vivid English printed
cottons were used to make the quilt, including the green
and burnt orange rainbow fabric that serves as a background for each Mariner's Compass block. The backing is of
a blue and white rainbow printed cotton. The quilting
follows the outline of each individual compass point.

1988.128   (catalogue no. 30)

Quilt, Pinwheel or Fly pattern

Maker unknown, Amish
Indiana, 1930
84 × 71 in.
Top: wool; *back*: cotton; *binding*: self-bound, back turned over
   front and stitched
Inscribed (quilted in each corner, counterclockwise): *JL[?]/
   Jan/23/1930*
Friends of the American Wing Fund, 1988

The black wool ground fabric sets off the brightly colored
pieced blocks of this quilt. It has a maroon and beige
inner border and a plain black outer border that is quilted
with fiddlehead fern motifs. The plain black blocks
that alternate with the pieced blocks are quilted with feather
wreaths. The backing is of a blue cotton fabric.

Publication: Bishop 1975, pl. 88.

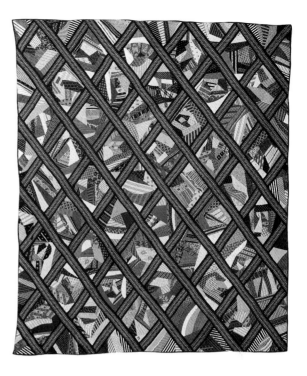

1988.213   (catalogue no. 37)

Doll Quilt, Chimney Sweep pattern

Ella Mygatt Whittlesey (about 1845–?)
United States, 1852
26 × 24¾ in.
Top: cotton; *back*: cotton; *binding*: cotton
Inscribed (in ink on back): *ELLA MYgatt WhittLESEY/AGED
    SEVEN. HER "stint"/Taught by heR GRANDMotheR
    ELINOR STUART./1852.*
Purchase, Mrs. Roger Brunschwig Gift, 1988

This small quilt has nine blocks in the Chimney Sweep
pattern. The blocks are pieced of plain white woven cotton
and calico printed in shades of brown, red, and orange. The
backing is also of white cotton, while the edge binding is of
a more tightly woven white cotton. The piece is completely
hand stitched, and it is quilted in parallel lines in the plain
areas and in a large diamond grid in the pieced blocks.

1989.27   (catalogue no. 32)

Quilt, Contained Crazy pattern

Nancy Doughty (about 1790–?)
Probably Maryland, 1872
89½ × 72 in.
Top: cotton; *back*: cotton; *binding*: cotton
Inscribed (in ink on center piece of striped fabric): *Made
    by/Mrs. Nancy Doughty/in the/82nd year of her age/for her
    friend/Miss Lizzie Cole. A. D. 1872*; in crayon or wax pencil
    on back: *3 3 + 5 5*
Purchase, Mr. and Mrs. Edward Scheider Gift, 1989

The diamond-shaped Crazy blocks of this quilt are pieced of
a variety of brown, orange, and pink printed cottons. The
blocks are joined together with brown and black printed
cotton sashing. The blocks are stitched to the sashing by
sewing machine; the remainder of the quilt is hand stitched.
The backing fabric is of a white cotton printed with a small
brown grid. The piece is quilted over its entire surface with
diagonal parallel lines.

Publication: Peck 1989, p. 61.
Reference: McMorris 1984.

1989.66   (catalogue no. 33)

Quilt Top, Crazy pattern

Maker unknown
New York State, about 1885
60¾ × 52 in.
Front: silk, satin, ribbons, and cotton velvets with silk and cotton
    embroidery; *back*: pieces stitched onto heavily starched
    cotton
Gift of Tracey Blumenreich Zabar, 1989

This multicolored, extensively decorated Crazy quilt top is
made up of pieced blocks that have been hand stitched
together, six blocks across by seven blocks down. The piece
is embroidered and appliquéd with many designs, including cats, butterflies, a horse, fans, and other Japanese and
Chinese motifs. The quilt top was left unfinished; it has
never been lined or quilted.

Reference: McMorris 1984.

1989.255   (catalogue no. 38)

Crib Quilt, Mill Wheel pattern

Maker unknown
Pennsylvania, about 1840
44 × 40¾ in.
Top: cotton; *back*: cotton; *binding*: cotton
Friends of the American Wing Fund, 1989

The front of this crib quilt is pieced of printed red cotton
with a green figure and plain white cotton fabric. The edge
binding is a different red printed cotton. The backing fabric
is the same white cotton that was used for piecing the front.
The quilt is entirely hand stitched and is quilted following
the pieced pattern.

38.59   (catalogue no. 1)

Coverlet, Pictorial pattern

Probably Sarah Furman Warner Williams
New York City, about 1803
103¼ × 90½ in.
Top: linen with linen and cotton appliqués, silk embroidery
    thread; *back*: linen; *binding*: self-bound, edges turned into
    each other and stitched together
Inscribed (in silk embroidery thread): *P W*
Gift of Catharine E. Cotheal, 1938

The coverlet's linen ground is appliquéd with linen and
cotton and embroidered with silk. The piece is decorated
with a complex design of a central vase of flowers on a
landscape decorated with people and animals. There is an
appliquéd floral border. The appliqués that are not figures
cut from chintz are embroidered in silk with buttonhole
stitch. The coverlet is neither filled nor quilted; the top is
attached to the back at the edges and also by one row of
stitching about two inches in from the edge.

Publications: Bordes 1974, no. 1; Cavallo 1979, pp. 36–37;
Downs 1938, pp. 180–82; Orlofsky 1974, pl. 66; Robertson
1948, p. 117; Safford and Bishop 1972, p. 12.
References: Swan 1976; Swan 1977.

38.115.1

Quilt, Prairie Flower pattern

Maker unknown
Virginia, about 1840
108½ × 107¼ in.
Top: cotton; *back*: cotton; *binding*: cotton
Gift of Frances T. Stockwell, 1938

The top of the quilt is composed of sixteen blocks of finely
woven white cotton, each appliquéd with flowers that have
red and pink printed cotton petals and green leaves. The
back is of a more coarsely woven white cotton, and the
binding is of a red plaid cotton. The piece is quilted with a
pattern of roundels and leaf sprays.

Publications: Downs 1938, pp. 180–82; Ickis 1959, pp. 112–14;
Orlofsky 1974, p. 295.

Notes: Although family history relates that this quilt is
made completely of cotton that was grown, spun, and
woven in Virginia, some of the fabrics used in the appliqués
are English.

38.115.2

Quilt, Floral pattern

Possibly Eliza Armstead Miller
Virginia, about 1795
94½ × 72½ in.
Top: cotton; *back*: cotton; *binding*: self-bound, edges turned
    into each other and stitched together
Inscribed (embroidered in blue thread): *E A M* (only *E* is still
    visible)
Gift of Frances T. Stockwell, 1938

The quilt is decorated with an appliquéd central basket of
flowers surrounded by two vine borders. The vines are of
blue cotton with chintz flowers and leaves in shades of
pink, blue, and brown. Each piece of appliqué is stitched
down with white cotton thread in the herringbone stitch.
The piece is quilted in an overall diamond grid.

Publications: Downs 1938, pp. 180–82; Orlofsky 1974, pl. 38;
Robertson 1948, p. 122.

Notes: This quilt is in poor condition, primarily due to the
cleaning and attempted repair that took place in 1962. Many
of the original appliquéd fabrics have been removed, and
only the *E* of the embroidered initials remains intact. The
bottom strip of the quilt is a twentieth-century addition,
most likely made after the piece entered the Museum. A
1950s photo of the quilt on a bed in one of our period rooms
clearly shows that the bottom strip was added so that the
quilt would fit the bed correctly.

45.38   (catalogue no. 36)

Crib Quilt, *Alice in Wonderland* pattern

Designed by Marion Cheever Whiteside Newton (?–1965)
New York City, 1945
65⅝ × 45 in.
Top: cotton; *back*: cotton; *binding*: cotton
Inscribed (embroidered in chain stitch at bottom left cor-
    ner): *1945/Marion Whiteside Newton*
Purchase, Edward C. Moore, Jr. Gift, 1945

Blocks of yellow printed cotton alternate with appliquéd
blocks showing scenes from Lewis Carroll's *Alice in Wonderland* on this crib quilt. The appliquéd blocks include multicolored and patterned fabrics, and some of the details are in
stem-stitch embroidery. The blocks are machine stitched
together, but the appliqué work and quilting are done by
hand. The piece is diamond quilted overall in a four-inch grid.

References: Anderson 1944; Benberry 1986.

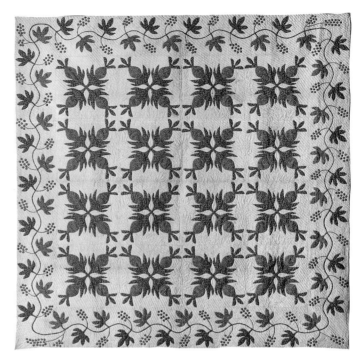

52.103 (catalogue no. 18)

Quilt, Album pattern

Members of the First Reformed Churches of Fishkill and
  Hopewell, Dutchess County, New York, about 1855–60
83½ × 84½ in.
Top: cotton; *back*: cotton; *binding*: cotton
Inscribed (in ink): *Miss Sarah Pollock, Mrs. Humphrey, Elizabeth
  Boice, Maria Husted, Susan Adriana Monfort, Miss Malinda
  Brewer, Miss Jane Rapalje, Mrs. E. Bogardus, H. E. Monfort,
  A.* [?], *Mrs. Thos. Adriance, Miss Annie* [?] *Clapp, Elizabeth
  Van Wyck*
Gift of Miss Eliza Polhemus Cobb, 1952

This appliquéd and pieced quilt has a white woven cotton
ground, solid red sashing, and designs appliquéd primarily
in red fabric in the blocks. Some blocks include solid blue-
green and green cottons. The swag border is made of red
calico. The white woven cotton binding is machine stitched.
The blocks are diamond quilted, the swag border is quilted
in curves that follow the swags, and the sashing is quilted
with parallel lines of stitching.

Reference: *Records of the First Reformed Church, Fishkill,
Dutchess County, New York* and *The First Reformed Church,
Hopewell, Dutchess County, New York*, 1981.

Notes: For placement of inscriptions, see diagram, p. 60.

56.179

Quilt, Pineapple pattern

Ann Downing Hegeman
Glen Head, Nassau County, New York, about 1865
93 × 91 in.
Top: cotton; *back*: cotton; *binding*: cotton
Gift of Mrs. J. Hoyt Kerley, 1956

The quilt top has twelve blocks appliquéd with red and
green calico pineapples. An appliquéd grapevine border
surrounds the entire field. The top and backing are of white
woven cotton, and there is a solid red cotton edge binding.
The appliqués are machine stitched on the broad parts of
the leaves and pineapples and hand stitched around the
grapes and thin stems. In addition to the finely quilted
diagonal parallel lines over most of the piece, leaf patterns
are quilted between the pineapple blocks.

Notes: According to the donor of this quilt, it was made by
Ann Downing Hegeman in about 1840 and given to her new
daughter-in-law, Sarah Ann Craft, on her marriage to Ann's
son Cornelius Hegeman on April 15, 1841. However, on
examination, it becomes evident that a sewing machine was
used to stitch down the broad areas of the appliqués. Since
the sewing machine was not invented until 1846, it is more
likely that the quilt was made a number of years later than
the date assigned to it by the donor.

1970.288   (catalogue no. 2)

Quilt, chintz appliquéd

Mary Malvina Cook Taft (1812–?)
Possibly Maryland, Virginia, or South Carolina, about 1830–35
110¼ × 92½ in.
Top: cotton; *back*: cotton; *binding*: cotton
Gift of Miss Elsey R. Taft, 1970

This white cotton quilt is appliquéd with a central chintz
rose bush growing from a basket of roses, tulips, and
other flowers. There are three borders, the central of chintz
fabric, the second appliquéd with birds, butterflies, palm
trees, and flowers, and the outermost of a small floral
border chintz. It is quilted overall in one-half-inch diamond
quilting, except for the two chintz borders, which are quilted
with diagonal parallel lines. The white cotton fabric of the
top is of a much finer weave than the white cotton backing.
The edges are bound with white cotton tape.

Reference: Allen 1987.

1971.180.123

Quilt, chintz appliquéd

Maker unknown
Maryland, about 1800
96¼ × 96½ in.
Top: cotton; *back*: cotton; *binding*: self-bound, edges turned
    into each other and stitched together
Bequest of Flora E. Whiting, 1971

This quilt has a central flowering tree of appliquéd chintz,
surrounded by appliquéd blue and pink calico vines, swags,
and sawtooth and scalloped borders. The outermost border
is shell quilted, while the inner area is quilted with roses,
leaves, vines, and grapes. There are some modern replace-
ments to the chintz areas. A cotton fringe is attached on
three sides. The back is of plain white woven cotton.

Publication: Bordes 1974, no. 2.
Reference: Peto 1939, pl. 1.

Notes: It is assumed that this quilt is from Maryland because of the existence of similar, well-documented examples from that state. A number of the chintzes used for
the appliqués can be documented to the period between
1780 and 1800. The piece is in very fragile condition and has
been extensively repaired over the years.

1971.180.126

Quilt, chintz appliquéd

Designed by Eleanor Beard (1891–1951)
Hardinsburg, Breckinridge County, Kentucky, about 1921–50
92 × 79½ in.
Top: cotton; *back*: cotton sateen; *binding*: self-bound, edges
 turned into each other and stitched together
Inscribed (on two woven labels attached to back at lower
 right corner): *Eleanor Beard/Hardinsburg, Ky.* and *THE
 MATERIAL/IN THIS ARTICLE/IS MADE OF/ALL COTTON*
Bequest of Flora E. Whiting, 1971

This quilt is formed of appliquéd chintz blocks with brown
and red printed calico sashing. The chintzes are of varying
ages; the oldest, a flower basket in the largest block, is from
approximately 1800, while the newest seems to be from the
first half of the twentieth century. The base onto which the
appliqués are stitched is of finely woven white cotton, and
the backing is of cotton sateen. The sashing is sewn to the
blocks by machine; the appliqués are all hand sewn, and
some are surrounded by either buttonhole or chain stitch.
The piece is hand quilted in diagonal parallel lines.

Reference: Benberry 1986.

Notes: Although this quilt copies an older model, it was
made in the first half of the twentieth century. Eleanor
Beard designed quilts for the successful Kentucky cottage
industry called Hedgelands Studio that she founded in
1921. By 1929, her quilts were sold in many American cities,
including New York and Chicago, at shops and through
representatives. She advertised her firm as creating "hand
quilted things for bedroom, boudoir, travel, etc." Many of
her designs had chintz appliqués, and one of her catalogues
mentioned that she was willing to work with chintz pieces
supplied by the client. It is quite possible that Mrs. Whiting,
the donor of this quilt, who was an avid antiques collector,
provided Eleanor Beard with the nineteenth-century fabrics
found appliquéd on the piece. Prices in one catalogue,
which probably dates from the 1940s, disclose that chintz
appliquéd quilts were about $250 each. When this quilt
came into the Museum's collection in 1971, it was assumed
that it was from the nineteenth century, but the growing
awareness of twentieth-century quilts made it possible to
discover its correct origin and date. The Eleanor Beard
Studio still exists in Hardinsburg and continues to make
bed covers as well as other quilted items.

1971.180.127

Quilt, Rose of Sharon pattern

Maker unknown
Possibly Pennsylvania, about 1860
83¾ × 84⁵⁄₁₆ in.
Top: cotton; *back*: cotton; *binding*: cotton
Bequest of Flora E. Whiting, 1971

The top of the quilt is of a white cotton fabric printed with a thin red stripe. The appliquéd flowers are of pink and green cotton. The edge binding is of green plaid cotton. White cotton fabric with a small dark red figure is used for the backing. There are large-scale quilted flower and feather forms in some areas, as well as an overall pattern of diagonal parallel lines.

Notes: The quilt is extremely worn and faded. There are breaks in the appliqué fabric and losses to the quilting.

1971.180.129

Quilt, Feathered Star pattern with chintz appliqués

Maker unknown
United States, about 1865
106 × 106¾ in.
Top: cotton; *back*: linen; *binding*: cotton
Bequest of Flora E. Whiting, 1971

The main ground of this quilt is dark blue calico pieced into feathered stars. The voids in between the stars are of white cotton fabric that has been appliquéd with a variety of flowers that have been cut from chintzes. The edging is of a second dark blue calico. The piece is decorated with very fine quilting in various grid and arc patterns and is completely hand stitched.

Notes: This quilt is in poor condition. It is stained, the chintz appliqués are faded, and there is overall yellowing.

1971.180.130

Quilt, chintz appliquéd

Maker unknown
Southern United States, about 1820–30
89½ × 88¾ in.
Top: linen and cotton; *back*: linen; *binding*: linen
Bequest of Flora E. Whiting, 1971

The quilt top, binding, and backing are made from white
linen fabric. The top is decorated with chintz appliqués
and a chintz border. The central floral medallion and the
four corner ovals are printed in shades of pink, red, brown,
and blue-green. The chintz border is printed with roses on a
vermicelli background. There are fine double shells quilted
in the central area and parallel diagonal lines quilted in
the border.

Reference: Allen 1987.

Notes: The Textile Study Room at the Metropolitan has an
uncut panel printed with the four corner floral ovals
(accession no. 26.189.14). This panel can be dated to about
1815 and has remained very freshly colored over time. On
the panel, the oval is surrounded by four triangular floral
sprays, which are stitched together on this quilt into hour-
glass or butterfly forms. The chintz border fabric is probably
from the 1830s. The quilt is in poor condition; it is stained
and faded.

1974.24   (catalogue no. 16)

Quilt, Presentation pattern

Probably Mary Evans (1829–1916)
Baltimore, Maryland, about 1849
106¼ × 103¾ in.
Top: cotton and silk velvet; *back*: cotton; *binding*: cotton
Inscribed (embroidered on book in center block): *BIBLE*; (in
    ink in basket blocks, clockwise from top): *Chine'es basket/
    Swiss basket/Wicker basket/Rustic basket*; (in ink in musical
    trophy block): *sacred ___ies*
Sansbury-Mills Fund, 1974

The twenty-nine ornately appliquéd blocks of this quilt
display intricately designed floral wreaths and bouquets,
baskets of various styles, birds, fruit, and musical instru-
ments. The blocks are of differing sizes: The center block is
four times the size of the outer blocks and is surrounded by
four blocks that are double the size of the outer blocks. The
white cotton ground fabric is quilted overall in a diamond
pattern, and each appliquéd piece is quilted around its
edges. There is a plain patch of white cotton fabric under
the central basket.

Publications: Bordes 1974, no. 6; Katzenberg 1981, no. 19.
Reference: Dunton 1946.

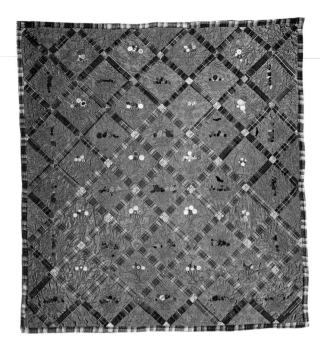

1975.95   (catalogue no. 22)

Quilt, Fruit Baskets pattern

Maker unknown
Possibly Providence, Rhode Island, about 1860
86 × 79 in.
Top: silk and silk velvet; *back*: silk; *binding*: silk
Gift of Mr. and Mrs. Samuel Schwartz, 1975

This silk quilt is both pieced and appliquéd. Each lead-gray
diamond-shaped block is decorated with either a quilted
epergne or a basket onto which velvet fruits and flowers
have been appliquéd. The blocks are separated by sashing
of brightly colored plaid taffeta. The back is made from
white silk and has an appliquéd block at each corner.

1988.24.2   (catalogue no. 14)

Quilt, Oak Leaf pattern

Maker unknown
Possibly Rhinebeck, Dutchess County, New York,
   about 1860
93½ × 76½ in.
Top: cotton; *back*: cotton; *binding*: cotton
Purchase, Mrs. Roger Brunschwig Gift, 1988

The plain white cotton fabric top of this quilt is appliquéd
with a dark blue cotton printed with a small white
figure. The twelve oak leaf blocks are separated by sashing
cut from the same blue fabric, and the wide border is
decorated with hearts and flowers. The blue fabric is also
used for the edge binding. The back is of plain white woven
cotton. The piece is finely quilted along the edges of the
appliquéd oak leaves and border figures and in parallel
lines following the outlines of the figures in the white
areas.

1988.134   (catalogue no. 17)

Quilt, Album pattern

Members of the Brown and Turner families
Baltimore, Maryland, begun in 1846
83⅜ × 85 in.
Top: cotton; *back*: cotton; *binding*: self-bound, back turned
  over front and stitched
Inscribed (in ink in each block, starting at top left): *Elizabeth
  Morrison; Margaret L. Brown/March 18th 1847; Ann Brown/
  Baltimore/January 29th 1847; Rachel D. Taylor/May 1847;
  M. A. Hook* [in cross-stitch]; *Elizabeth D. Dobler/1847;
  Jane L. Creamer/Baltimore/Dec. 15, 1846;* [unmarked block];
  *Helen Brown/ Baltimore/January 29th 1846; Mary Turner/March
  18th 1847;* [unmarked block]; *Francis Turner/March 2 1847;
  Mary Ann O'Laughlen/1846; Mary A. Dobler; M A H/1852*
  [in cross-stitch]; *Frances Leivis (?)/Susan I. Turner/Baltimore/*

*March 18th 1847; Jane Brown/ March 6th 1847; Agnes A. S.
  House/March 8th 1847;* [unmarked block]; *Mary E. Doretee/
  March 9th 1847; Susan Amanda Turner; May 13; Presented by
  M. W. Conal*[?] [in cross-stitch]/*1846; Mary E. Turner/March
  9th 1847; Susanna Turner/March 1st 1847*
Bequest of Margaret Brown Potvin, 1987

Appliquéd with various floral and abstract designs, the
twenty-five blocks of this quilt are separated by red cotton
sashing. The designs in the blocks are cut from fabrics
primarily in shades of red and green. All the blocks are
hand stitched and signed by different hands, some in ink,
some in cross-stitch. The blocks are joined to the sashing by
sewing machine. The back is of plain white woven cotton.

Publication: Peck 1988, p. 59.
References: Dunton 1946; Katzenberg 1981.

10.125.413

Coverlet, whole-cloth

Maker unknown
United States, about 1830
93¼ × 87¾ in.
Top (only): cotton
Inscribed: (printed on fabric in central medallion):
    ANDREW JACKSON / MAGNANIMOUS IN PEACE / VIC-
TORIOUS IN WAR; (in circle around portrait): PRESIDENT
OF THE UNITED STATES FROM MARCH 4th 1829 TO ~
SUPREME COMMANDER OF THE ARMY & NAVY.
Underneath portraits of Presidents (from left to right):
THOMAS JEFFERSON / PRESIDENT FROM 1801 TO
1809; JOHN Q ADAMS / PRESIDENT FROM 1825 TO
1829; JAMES MONROE / PRESIDENT FROM 1817 TO
1825; WASHINGTON / PRESIDENT FROM 1789 TO 1797;
JAMES MADISON / PRESIDENT FROM 1809 TO 1817;
JOHN ADAMS / PRESIDENT FROM 1797 TO 1801. On
ribbon draped around eagle: E PLURIBUS UNUM
Gift of Mrs. Russell Sage, 1909

This coverlet consists of four panels of green printed cotton stitched together. Two are full panels, each measuring twenty-five inches selvedge to selvedge. The piece has no filling, backing, or binding. The top and bottom edges of the corner ends of the piece are partially machine stitched, and one side is unfinished and has a torn edge.

References: Collins 1979, no. 70; Montgomery 1970, p. 341; The New-York Historical Society (exhib. cat.) 1941, no. 110.

Notes: The fabric that was stitched together to make this coverlet was roller printed in England for the American market. It was probably adapted from an earlier French copperplate-printed cotton fabric that did not include the portrait of Andrew Jackson or the frigate *Constitution*. Other examples of this fabric, including two in the Metropolitan's Textile Study Room (accession nos. 26.365.48 and 48.164.3), have been found printed in shades of blue, pink, and brown. Although this piece was accessioned in 1909 as a bed cover, the fabric may not have been used for that purpose originally. The piece is in poor condition; it has many stains and is faded overall.

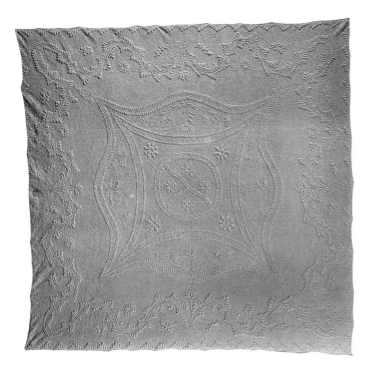

40.71

Quilt, whole-cloth whitework

Maria Kellogg Richards
Probably Norwalk, Fairfield County, Connecticut,
  about 1805
96 × 94⅝ in.
Top: cotton; *back*: cotton; *binding*: cotton tape
Gift of Mrs. Laura W. Merrill, Mrs. Mabel W. Powell, and
  Mrs. Alice W. Ferres, 1940

The top of this white quilt is made of tightly woven cotton,
while the backing fabric is of a coarser woven cotton. The
tape binding is probably handwoven. The decoratively
patterned areas are stuffed with wool. The piece is quilted
with a central squared medallion that has a pineapple at
each of the four corners. The feather-vine border terminates
in the mid-point of each of the four sides with a flower tied
with a bow.

Notes: According to family history, this quilt was made by
Maria Kellogg and her sisters as a gift for their mother,
Lydia Bouton Kellogg. The quilt was passed down to Maria
after her marriage to Daniel Richards and then through
succeeding generations until 1940, when it was given to the
Museum by Maria Kellogg's great-granddaughters, Laura
Whiton Merrill, Mabel Whiton Powell, and Alice Whiton
Ferres. For an interesting comparison, see our loom-woven
Marseilles quilt (catalogue no. 47).

44.42   (catalogue no. 44)

Coverlet, whole-cloth stenciled

Maker unknown
Probably New York State, about 1820–40
89 × 81 in.
Top (only): cotton
Rogers Fund, 1944

This one-layer coverlet is made of three lengths of white
cotton fabric that are seamed together. Red, yellow, and
green paints are stenciled on the surface in a pattern of nine
medallions with a surrounding border of flowers, fruit, and
birds.

Publication: Winchester 1945, p. 145.
Reference: Howe 1940, pp. 120–22.

45.107

Quilt, whole-cloth calimanco

Maker unknown
New England, about 1750
102½ × 99½ in.
Top: wool; *back*: cotton; *binding*: self-bound, front turned
over back and stitched
Rogers Fund, 1945

The top of this quilt is of a rust-colored glazed wool, and the
back is of a coarsely woven gold cotton. The top is made of
three panels of fabric, the widest 37½ inches. The piece is
quilted with a central area of quatrefoils, a feather-vine
border, and pyramids of shells.

Reference: Montgomery 1984, pp. 185–87.

Notes: The asymmetry and disorganization of the quilting
on this piece are quite unusual. For other examples of
calimanco (a type of plain-weave glazed wool) quilts in
the American Wing's collection, see catalogue no. 42 and
accession nos. 62.26 and 1980.454 (pp. 222 and 225,
respectively).

45.145   (catalogue no. 41)

Quilt, whole-cloth

Maker unknown
Probably English, about 1790
97 × 77½ in.
Top: cotton; *back*: cotton; *binding*: self-bound, edges
turned into each other and stitched together
Gift of Mrs. Frederick H. Getman, in memory of her
husband, 1945

Both the front and back of this whole-cloth quilt are constructed of three panels of approximately twenty-six-inch-
width fabric that have been stitched together. The front is
copperplate printed with blue floral vines on a white ground,
and the back is a red copperplate scenic print on a white
ground. The piece is quilted in various fan and diamond
patterns in borders around a diamond-quilted central panel.

References: Floud 1956, p. 127; Montgomery 1970, fig. 235;
The Victoria and Albert Museum (exhib. cat.) 1955, no. 10.

Back of 45.145   (catalogue no. 41)

58.41   (catalogue no. 42)

Quilt, whole-cloth calimanco

Maker unknown
Possibly New York State, about 1780–1800
96¼ × 90½ in.
Top: wool; *back*: wool; *binding*: wool
Inscribed (quilted under central medallion): *L M & W D* [?]
Rogers Fund, 1958

This quilt has a rust-colored glazed wool top and back, with brick-red wool edge binding. It is quilted with a central medallion and a feather-vine border.

Reference: Montgomery 1984, pp. 185–87.

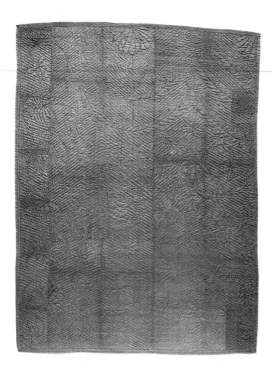

62.26

Quilt, whole-cloth calimanco

Maker unknown
Possibly Massachusetts, about 1775–90
95¼ × 70½ in.
Top: wool; *back*: wool; *binding*: wool
Rogers Fund, 1962

The top of this quilt is of a glazed indigo-blue wool, while the backing is of a more coarsely woven unglazed golden-brown wool. The edge binding and the top are both made from the same indigo-blue wool. The piece is quilted in a design of scrolls, flowers, and leaf sprays against a diagonally quilted ground.

References: Montgomery 1984, pp. 185–87; Wadsworth Atheneum (exhib. cat.) 1985, no. 248.

Inst.63.7.10   (catalogue no. 40)

Quilt, whole-cloth

Maker unknown
England or United States, about 1835
81¾ × 90½ in.
Top: cotton; *back*: cotton; *binding*: cotton tape
Gift of Mr. and Mrs. Harcourt Amory, 1963

This chintz quilt is notched at its bottom corners to accommodate bedposts. The quilt is bound with cotton tape striped in tan, white, black, and blue. The chintz top fabric is decorated with floral trails, roller printed in red and block overprinted in blue, yellow, and green on a tan ground. The backing chintz has a floral stripe, roller printed in red and brown. The piece is quilted overall with a shell pattern.

Reference: Montgomery 1970, figs. 332, 333.

Back of Inst. 63.7.10   (catalogue no. 40)

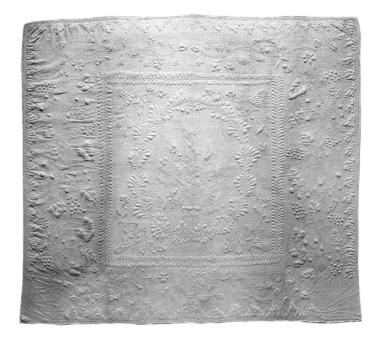

63.115

Quilt, whole-cloth whitework

Sarah Cook
Litchfield, Litchfield County, Connecticut, about 1800–1820
94¾ × 70½ in.
Top: cotton; *back*: cotton; *binding*: cotton tape
Gift of Mrs. Robert Bull, 1963

This white cotton quilt is decorated with corded, quilted, and stuffed motifs. The top fabric is more tightly woven than the backing cotton. At the center, there is a vase of flowers within an oval feather wreath, and the central field is surrounded by a wide border with rose and grape vines stemming from an urn at the bottom center. The two corners at the foot were left unquilted, probably because they were meant to be cut back to fit around bedposts.

Notes: This is a fairly typical example of an early-nineteenth-century Connecticut whitework quilt. Some of the quilt stitching on the piece is beginning to deteriorate.

Inst.67.2.3

Coverlet, whole-cloth

Maker unknown
England or United States, about 1835
93½ × 82¼ in.
Top: cotton; *back*: cotton; *binding*: cotton tape
Inscribed (printed in lozenge-shaped cartouche on back):
    W. CONNOR
Gift of Mrs. Samuel Schwartz, 1967

The coverlet top is of a glazed floral chintz; it has a beige
ground printed with red, blue, and yellow flowers and
green foliage. The back is randomly pieced of two chintzes
and two brown and red calicos. A piece of the same chintz
used for the top is pieced into the back and is inscribed with
the fabric printer's name. The edges of the top and back are
bound together with striped tape. The coverlet has no
batting between the top and back layers and is not quilted.

Notes: The top fabric of this coverlet can be dated to the
1830s and is typical of many floral patterns that were printed
in naturalistic colors on what Florence Montgomery, in her
1970 book *Printed Textiles*, calls "fancy machine grounds."
This coverlet was originally acquired by the Museum for
the fabric alone and was to be cut up and used for upholstery purposes; for this reason, it is identified by an instal-
lation number.

1971.180.124   (catalogue no. 43)

Quilt, whole-cloth whitework

Maker unknown
Probably Colchester, New London County, Connecticut,
    about 1810–15
102¾ × 103 in.
Top: cotton; *back*: cotton; *binding*: cotton
Bequest of Flora E. Whiting, 1971

The top of this white cotton quilt is of a tightly woven white
cotton. There are two layers of backing, a very coarsely
woven layer and a less coarse show layer. The edge is bound
with cotton twill tape. The piece is patterned with a central
basket of flowers surrounded by four different ornate borders. The quilting is extremely fine; the patterned areas
have been stuffed for stronger definition.

Reference: Safford and Bishop 1972, p. 83.

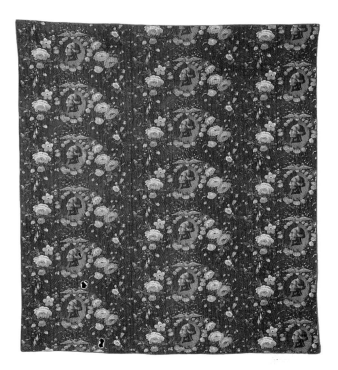

1980.454

Quilt, whole-cloth calimanco

Maker unknown
Great Britain or America, about 1780
98¼ × 79½ in.
Top: wool; *back*: wool; *binding*: self-bound, edges turned
into each other and stitched together
Sansbury-Mills Fund, 1980

The top, back, filling, and quilting thread of this calimanco quilt are all made of wool fibers. The top is of a glazed red wool; the back, of a tan unglazed wool; the quilting thread is dyed red-orange. The top is composed of four lengths of fabric, stitched together horizontally. The piece is decorated with a central diamond-quilted panel, with surrounding borders in diamond, fan, and circular patterns.

Reference: Montgomery 1984, pp. 185–87.

Notes: The quilting patterns found on this work indicate a possible British origin. This type of quilt could have been exported ready-made to the United States during the eighteenth century.

1985.347   (catalogue no. 45)

Quilt, whole-cloth

Maker unknown
United States, about 1876
89½ × 79½ in.
Top: cotton; *back*: cotton; *binding*: cotton tape
Inscribed (printed in each George Washington medallion):
WASHINGTON and INDEPENDENCE/4th July 1776
Gift of Helen W. Hughart, 1985

The front and back of this whole-cloth quilt are constructed of two complete width and one cut-width lengths of fabric seamed at their selvedges. The front is a multicolored roller-printed cotton showing medallions with trompe-l'oeil relief busts of George Washington. Each medallion is topped with an eagle and surrounded with a wreath of flowers. The back is of a dark brown calico with a lozenge design in brown and red. The piece is fan quilted overall.

References: Collins 1979, fig. 394; Montgomery 1970, fig. 406.

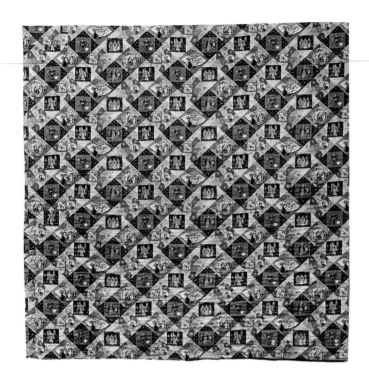 

1986.342   (catalogue no. 46)

Back of 1986.342   (catalogue no. 46)

Quilt, whole-cloth

Maker unknown
New England, about 1886
88¾ × 85¼ in.
Top: cotton; *back*: cotton; *binding*: self-bound, edges turned
    into each other and stitched together
Inscribed (front): various descriptive sentences about the
    illustrated scenes from *The Mikado*; (back): names of the
    illustrated yachts
Gift of Reginald Allen, 1986

Both the front and back of this whole-cloth quilt are constructed of four panels of fabric, which are stitched together
by sewing machine. Three of the panels are approximately
twenty-four inches wide each, and the partial last panel is
eleven inches wide. The front is printed with a trompe-l'oeil
patchwork in red, browns, and pink and shows scenes from
Gilbert and Sullivan's operetta *The Mikado*. The back is
printed with a trompe-l'oeil Crazy patchwork illustrating
the yachts in the 1886 America's Cup race. The quilt is
knotted through the two fabric layers and the cotton batting
with heavy white cotton thread in eight-inch intervals; the
knots are at the corners of the diamond-shaped ''blocks'' in
the Mikado pattern.

References: Affleck 1987; Burke et al. 1986, p. 94.

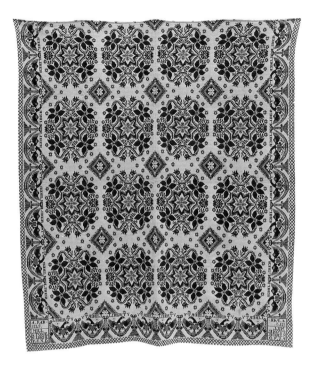

10.125.407

Coverlet, Lilies of France pattern with Eagle and *Liberty* borders

Peter Sutphen Van Doren (1806–1899)
Millstone, Somerset County, New Jersey, 1838
Made for A. Parsils
97½ × 77 in.
Double cloth, woven on a hand loom with attached Jacquard
    mechanism; *warp*: cotton and wool; *weft*: cotton and wool
Inscribed (in two bottom corner blocks, right block in re-
    verse): *A. PAR -/SILS./MILL/STONE./NJ. 1838/P.S.V.D.*
Gift of Mrs. Russell Sage, 1909

Undyed cotton and dark blue wool are woven together to
form this coverlet. The field has repeating floral medallions,
and the border has emblematic eagles in tassel-and-swag
borders, with *LIBERTY* woven forward and in reverse above
each of their heads. The coverlet is woven in two panels and
seamed at the center. It is unfringed.

References: Davison and Mayer-Thurman 1973, no. 147;
Heisey 1978, p. 113.

Notes: Peter Sutphen Van Doren was one of a family of
weavers. He had three brothers: Isaac William, Abram
William, and Garret William. For a time, they all wove in
Millstone, New Jersey, but in 1838, Abram William went
West to work as a weaver in Oakland County, Michigan. All
the other Van Doren brothers seem to have stayed in New
Jersey. Coverlets woven by Peter Sutphen that date between
1838 and 1846 have been found.

10.125.408

Coverlet, plaid

Maker unknown
Probably Pennsylvania, about 1840
106½ × 84½ in.
Woven on a hand loom; *warp*: wool; *weft*: wool
Gift of Mrs. Russell Sage, 1909

This plaid coverlet is woven of brown, blue, yellow, and
orange wool in two panels and seamed at the center. It has a
natural fringe along the bottom.

References: Burnham 1972, pp. 114–17; Davison and Mayer-
Thurman 1973, nos. 35–37.

Notes: There are three plaid bed coverings similar to this
one in the collection of the Art Institute of Chicago that are
documented to Pennsylvania or Ohio.

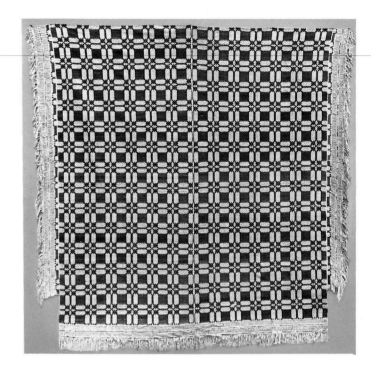

10.125.409

Coverlet, Saint Ann's Robe or Governor's Garden pattern

Maker unknown
United States, about 1825
92½ × 91 in.
Overshot, woven on a hand loom; *warp*: cotton; *weft*: cotton and wool
Gift of Mrs. Russell Sage, 1909

This overshot coverlet is woven of undyed cotton and dark blue wool in two panels and seamed at the center. A woven fringe was added on three sides.

References: Colonial Coverlet Guild of America 1940, p. 57; Hall 1912, p. 242.

Notes: This pattern, called Saint Ann's Robe or Governor's Garden in America, is also found in Canada. In their survey of Canadian coverlet weaving, *'Keep me warm one night'* (p. 248), Dorothy and Harold Burnham publish this pattern as "Indian Review." Our coverlet is finished on three sides with a particularly attractive added fringe, which is woven with the same pattern as the coverlet.

10.125.410   (catalogue no. 49)

Coverlet

Maker unknown
Probably Pennsylvania, about 1825
99½ × 102 in.
Overshot, woven on a hand loom; *warp*: cotton; *weft*: cotton and wool
Gift of Mrs. Russell Sage, 1909

This overshot coverlet is woven of undyed cotton and blue and orange wool in two panels and seamed at the center. There is an applied woven fringe along each side and along the bottom edge. The piece is T-shaped to accommodate bedposts.

13.84

Coverlet, Four Snowballs pattern with Pine-tree border

Maker unknown
Possibly Pennsylvania, about 1830
77¾ × 65¼ in.
Double cloth, woven on a hand loom; *warp*: cotton and wool; *weft*: cotton and wool
Gift of Mrs. Emerson Opdycke, in memory of her mother, 1913

This double cloth coverlet is woven in two panels from undyed cotton and dark blue, light blue, and salmon-colored wool. It is seamed at the center and hemmed at the top. The bottom edge is finished with a natural fringe.

14.22.1   (catalogue no. 57)

Coverlet

Peter Leisey (1802–1859)
Cocalico Township, Lancaster County, Pennsylvania, about 1835–50
108 × 81½ in.
Tied *Biederwand*, woven on a hand loom with an attached Jacquard mechanism; *warp*: cotton; *weft*: cotton and wool
Inscribed (in two bottom corner blocks, right block in reverse): *MADE/BY/PETER/LEISEY/LANCAS/TER. CO/ COCALECO/THOWNSHIP* [sic]
Rogers Fund, 1914

This coverlet is woven of blue cotton and red-orange wool in two panels and seamed at the center. The central field is decorated with rose clusters, large oak leaves, and acorn compass motifs. The pattern on the side borders depicts houses alternating with palm trees. The bottom edge has a signed block at each corner and a grapevine at its center. The left and right sides of the coverlet have natural fringe, and there is applied fringe along the bottom edge.

References: Allen 1986; Heisey 1978, p. 81; Philadelphia Museum of Art (exhib. cat.) 1984, no. 4E12.

14.22.2

Coverlet

Maker unknown
Probably Berks County, Pennsylvania, about 1840
98½ × 89¾ in.
Tied *Biederwand*, woven on a hand loom with an attached
   Jacquard mechanism; *warp*: cotton; *weft*: cotton and wool
Rogers Fund, 1914

This coverlet is woven in two panels and seamed at the
center. It has a warp of undyed and light blue cotton and a
weft of dark blue, green, and red wool and undyed cotton.
The central field shows feather medallions alternating with
foliate medallions. The bottom border has a stylized vine
motif, and the right and left borders have roses and tulips.
Peacocks adorn each of the two corner blocks. Both sides of
the coverlet have natural fringe, and there is attached fringe
along the bottom edge.

Reference: Allen 1986.

25.127   (catalogue no. 53)

Coverlet, Agriculture & Manufactures pattern

Maker unknown
Probably Ulster County, New York, 1837
Made for Phoebe Tilson
103¾ × 79¾ in.
Double cloth, woven on a hand loom with an attached
   Jacquard mechanism; *warp*: cotton and wool; *weft*: cotton
   and wool
Inscribed (in each of the four corner blocks): *AGRICUL/
TURE. & MAN/UFACTURES./ARE. THE. FOUND/ATION.
OF/OUR. INDE/PENDENCE./JULY. 4./1837*; (along top
and bottom, four times in two pairs, first of each pair in
reverse): *P. TILSON*
Gift of Mrs. Laura Tillson Vail, 1925

This double cloth coverlet is woven in one wide panel of
undyed cotton and dark blue wool. The central field has
large floral medallions, and the borders are decorated with
images of eagles with outspread wings alternating with
Masonic symbols.

Reference: Allen 1985.

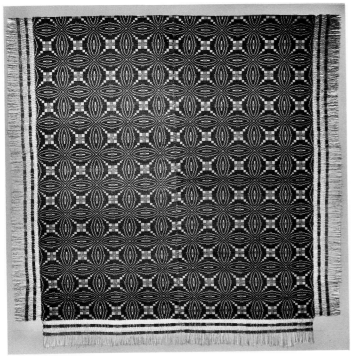

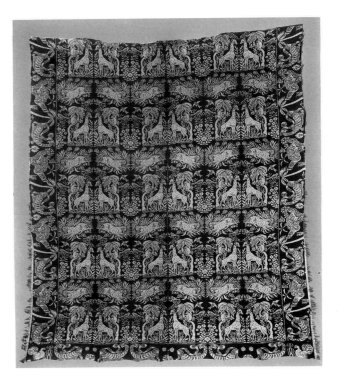

30.120.377   (catalogue no. 50)

Coverlet, Wheel of Fortune pattern variation

Maker unknown
United States, about 1820
104 × 104 in.
Summer and Winter, woven on a hand loom; *warp*: cotton;
    weft: cotton and wool
The Sylmaris Collection, Gift of George Coe Graves, 1930

This Summer and Winter coverlet is woven of undyed
cotton and dark blue wool in two panels and seamed at the
center. It has natural woven fringe along the bottom border
and applied woven fringe on the left and right sides.

Reference: Davison and Mayer-Thurman 1973, nos. 31–33.

56.113   (catalogue no. 59)

Coverlet

Possibly Mrs. Hicks
Probably Ohio, about 1850
85 × 73 in.
Double cloth, woven on a hand loom with an attached
    Jacquard mechanism; *warp*: wool; *weft*: wool
Rogers Fund, 1956

This coverlet is woven with red and blue wool warps and
red and blue wool wefts in two panels and seamed at the
center. The field shows a menagerie of animals, including
giraffes, leopards, monkeys, and birds. The borders have
images of an alligator eating a snake alternating with a
pouncing leopard. In contrast to the predominant jungle
motifs, domesticated fowl are depicted on the corner
blocks.

References: Davison and Mayer-Thurman 1973, no. 116;
Heisey 1978, p. 60; "Quilts and Coverlets" 1965.

Notes: The piece is in generally fair condition; however, the
fringed sides are ragged, and the top and bottom edges are
badly worn.

67.33 (catalogue no. 52)

Coverlet

Workshop of James Alexander (1770–1870)
Little Britain, Orange County, New York, 1828
Made for Mary Ann Wood
96¼ × 81 in.
Double cloth, probably woven on a drawloom; *warp*: cotton
  and wool; *weft*: cotton and wool
Inscribed (in each of the four corner blocks): *MARY ANN/*
  WOOD/DEC. 4/1828
Gift of Roger MacLaughlin, 1967

This dark blue wool and undyed cotton double cloth coverlet
is woven in two panels and seamed at the center. It has large
floral medallions in the center and borders of eagles with
outspread wings alternating with Masonic symbols. The
eagles on the top and bottom edges are more clumsily
designed than those along the right and left sides.

References: Allen 1985; Craft and Folk Art Museum (exhib.
cat.) 1976, no. 16; Heisey 1978, p. 31; Parslow 1956; Peck 1930;
Shaeffer, Partridge, and Adrosko 1985, pl. 1.

1973.74

Coverlet

Maker unknown
Probably New York State, 1833
Made for Phebe H. Foss
98½ × 74¼ in.
Double cloth, woven on a hand loom with an attached
  Jacquard mechanism; *warp*: cotton and wool; *weft*: cotton
  and wool
Inscribed (in each of the four corner blocks, each block
  made up of four smaller blocks with name woven for-
  ward, in reverse, and upside down): *Phebe/H Foss/ 1833*
Gift of Beatrice E. Noble, 1973

This dark blue wool and undyed cotton double cloth coverlet is woven in two panels and seamed at the center. It is
patterned with unusual floral medallions alternating with a
spoked wheel design. The border is decorated with a
simple design of repeating floral sprigs.

Notes: According to the donor, Phebe H. Foss may have
been her great-grandmother. Foss's family was from New
York State, but the specific county has not been ascertained.
The 1830 U.S. Census lists people named Foss in Dutchess,
Columbia, Oneida, Essex, and Steuben counties. Stylistically, the coverlet has much in common with other coverlets
documented to New York that have the same unusual four-
part corner blocks.

1982.243

Coverlet

Maker unknown
Probably Philadelphia, Pennsylvania, about 1876
86 × 80 in.
Tied *Biederwand*, woven on a power loom with an attached
    Jacquard mechanism; *warp*: cotton; *weft*: cotton and wool
Gift of Mr. and Mrs. John P. Kauffman, 1982

This red-orange wool and undyed and light blue cotton
coverlet is woven in one piece. There is a central star
medallion set in a scallop-patterned ground. The wide
borders are decorated with deer, partridges, foliage, and a
domed building. The work has a natural fringe on the left
and right sides and an added fringe along the bottom edge.

References: Burnham and Burnham 1972, no. 473; Shaeffer,
Partridge, and Adrosko 1985, p. 36.

Notes: This coverlet was passed down to one of the donors,
John P. Kauffman, from his grandmother Eva Derr Haag, of
Williamsport, Pennsylvania. The piece is typical of the last
cotton and wool woven coverlets made on power looms.
The weave is looser than the earlier Pennsylvania handwoven coverlets, and the red-orange aniline-dyed wool is
harshly colored. Coverlets such as these were often made as
souvenirs; this one may have been a memento of the 1876
Centennial Exposition in Philadelphia.

1982.366   (catalogue no. 56)

Coverlet

Maker unknown
Bergen County, New Jersey, or Rockland County, New York,
    1836
Made for Garret I. Smith
98 × 71½ in.
Double cloth, woven on a hand loom with an attached
    Jacquard mechanism; *warp*: wool; *weft*: wool
Inscribed (woven along top and bottom borders twice, both
    in reverse and forward): *GARRET/I. SMITH./1836.*
Dr. and Mrs. Kenneth H. Fried Gift and Friends of the
    American Wing Fund, 1982

This light and dark blue wool double cloth coverlet is woven
in two panels and seamed at the center. The ground is
decorated with various floral motifs associated with the
Dutch weavers of the Bergen County, New Jersey/Rockland
County, New York, area. The border is composed of birds
and tree motifs alternating with vases of flowers. Each of
the four corner blocks is decorated with a single large
sunflower. The piece has a natural fringe along the bottom.

Reference: ''Weavers of Bergen County'' 1983.

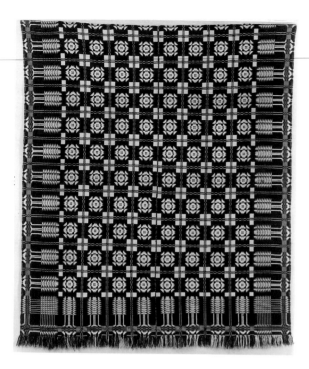

1984.330.1   (catalogue no. 51)

Coverlet, Virginia Beauty pattern with Pine-tree border

Maker unknown
Possibly New York, about 1825
91 × 75 in.
Double cloth, woven on a hand loom; *warp*: cotton and wool; *weft*: cotton and wool
Gift of Margaret and Richard Parrish, in memory of their paternal grandparents, Rebecca and Festus Parrish, 1984

This dark blue wool and undyed cotton double cloth coverlet is woven in two panels and seamed at the center. The coverlet's ground is geometrically patterned, and it has a pine-tree border. There is a natural fringe along the bottom edge.

1984.330.2   (catalogue no. 60)

Coverlet

Maker unknown
Possibly Indiana, about 1850
87½ × 81 in.
Double cloth, woven on a hand loom with an attached Jacquard mechanism; *warp*: cotton and wool; *weft*: cotton and wool
Gift of Margaret and Richard Parrish, in memory of their paternal grandparents, Rebecca and Festus Parrish, 1984

This double cloth coverlet is woven with undyed cotton and red and blue wool in two panels and seamed at the center. It is patterned with rows of floral clusters alternating with rows of single flowers, each within a cartouche. The piece is hemmed along the top border and has a natural fringe on the left and right sides and along the bottom edge.

1986.175 (catalogue no. 61)

Coverlet

Maker unknown
Made for Hannah Mariah Shelden (about 1824–?)
Washington Hollow (Dover District), Dutchess County,
 New York, 1844
80¼ × 103 in.
Double cloth, woven on a hand loom with an attached
 Jacquard mechanism; *warp*: cotton and wool; *weft*:
 cotton and wool
Inscribed (woven along top and bottom borders twice, both
 in reverse and forward): *HANNAH MARIAH SHELDEN
 AD 1844 WASHINGTON*
Gift of Hazel L. and Saidie E. Scudder, 1986

This red wool and undyed cotton double cloth coverlet is
woven in two panels and seamed at the center. It has a
central floral medallion and four large roses in the field. The
border has clusters of grapes and leaves, which alternate
with single-stemmed roses on the left and right sides and
with three snowflake motifs within the top and bottom
borders.

Reference: Safford and Bishop 1972, fig. 421.

1988.127 (catalogue no. 54)

Coverlet

David Daniel Haring (1800–1889)
Tappan Road, Harington Township, Bergen County,
 New Jersey, 1834
Made for Sarah Ann Outwater Verbryck (March 27, 1812–?)
98⅜ × 75 in.
Double cloth, woven on a hand loom with an attached
 Jacquard mechanism; *warp*: cotton and wool; *weft*: cotton
 and wool
Inscribed (in each of four cartouches, two at top and two at
 bottom, both in reverse and forward): *SARAH ANN/OUT-
 WATER/JAN 14 1834*; (beside each of the four corner
 blocks, left top and bottom in reverse): *(David D/Haring)/
 TAPPAN*
Purchase, Mrs. Roger Brunschwig Gift, 1988

This dark blue wool and undyed cotton double cloth coverlet
is woven in two panels and seamed at the center. Floral and
star motifs typically found in Haring's work decorate the
central field. The left and right borders have images of
eagles with outspread wings alternating with vases of
flowers and pairs of birds in trees. From left to right along
each panel of the top and bottom borders, there is a rooster
standing on an egg, the inscription cartouche, and an eagle.
The Haring trademark of a rose with four leaves on its stem
appears in each corner block. There is natural fringe along
the bottom edge.

References: Davison 1972; Davison and Mayer-Thurman
1973, no. 108; Heisey 1978, pp. 66–67; Moss 1975; "Weavers
of Bergen County" 1983.

1989.30   (catalogue no. 55)

Crib or Doll Coverlet

Probably David Daniel Haring (1800–1889)
Tappan Road, Harington Township, Bergen County,
    New Jersey, about 1832–38
Made for Rachel Blauvelt (1818–1899)
31¼ × 30½ in.
Double cloth, woven on a hand loom with an attached
    Jacquard mechanism; *warp*: cotton and wool; *weft*: cotton
    and wool
Inscribed (woven in two bottom corner blocks): *R + B*;
    (embroidered at lower left corner in white cotton
    thread): *B*
Purchase, Mrs. Roger Brunschwig Gift, 1989

This dark blue wool and undyed cotton double cloth crib or
doll coverlet is woven in one panel. Although the piece is
meant to be displayed with the two *R + B* blocks at the foot,
it is woven sideways. The natural fringes on the left and
right sides are the ends of the cut warp threads. The animal
and floral motifs are typical of Haring's work.

Publication: Peck 1989, p. 60.
References: Heisey 1978, pp. 66–67; Moss 1975; Ventre
1988; ''Weavers of Bergen County'' 1983.

1989.264.1   (catalogue no. 58)

Coverlet

Absalom Klinger (1817–1901)
Millersburg, Berks County, Pennsylvania, 1846
92½ × 89½ in.
Tied *Biederwand*, woven on a hand loom with an attached
    Jacquard mechanism; *warp*: cotton; *weft*: cotton and wool
Inscribed (in bottom two corner blocks, right block in
    reverse): *ABSALOM/KLINGER/MILLERS/BURG. BERKS/
    COUNTY,/1846/No 1687*
Gift of Mrs. James J. Rorimer, 1989

This coverlet is woven in one wide panel. The field is
decorated with quadrupled urns, and the left and right
borders show bowls of fruit. The piece is striped with bands
of medium blue, dark blue, and red wool. The undyed
cotton warp threads alternate with light blue cotton tie-
down threads. The piece is fringed on three sides; the two
side fringes are natural, and the fringe along the bottom is
attached.

Reference: Heisey 1978, p. 77.

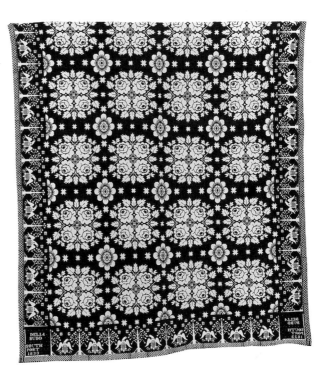

1989.264.2

Coverlet

Probably Asahel Phelps (1795–?)
Delhi, Delaware County, New York, 1853
100½ × 79¾ in.
Double cloth, woven on a hand loom with an attached
  Jacquard mechanism; *warp*: cotton and wool; *weft*: cotton
  and wool
Inscribed (in four corner blocks, under eagle): *DELHI.1853*
Gift of Mrs. James J. Rorimer, 1989

This dark blue wool and undyed cotton coverlet is woven
in two panels and seamed together at the center. The
central field is decorated with medallion forms. The wide
inner border shows floral and diamond motifs, while the
narrow outer border has alternating hearts and diamonds.
There are four corner blocks, each with an eagle surmounted
by thirteen stars.

Reference: Shaeffer, Partridge, and Adrosko 1985, pl. 14.

Notes: Asahel Phelps worked as a weaver in Delhi, Delaware County, between 1835 and 1854. He had a shop with
two looms, one for carpet and coverlet weaving and one for
plain weaving. He is listed as a farmer in the 1840 and 1850
United States Censuses, although his estate inventory clearly
shows that he maintained a weaving business as well.

1989.264.3

Coverlet

Maker unknown
Southport, Chemung County, New York, 1833
Made for Delia Budd
88 × 76¾ in.
Double cloth, woven on a hand loom with an attached
  Jacquard mechanism; *warp*: cotton and wool; *weft*: cotton
  and wool
Inscribed (in bottom two corner blocks, right block in re-
  verse): *DELIA/BUDD/SOUTH/PORT/1833*.
Gift of Mrs. James J. Rorimer, 1989

This dark blue wool and undyed cotton coverlet is woven in
two panels and seamed at the center. The central field is
patterned with quadrupled rose medallions, while the borders show alternating eagles and fruit trees.

Notes: The motifs found on this double cloth coverlet are
typical of coverlets woven in central and western New York
State.

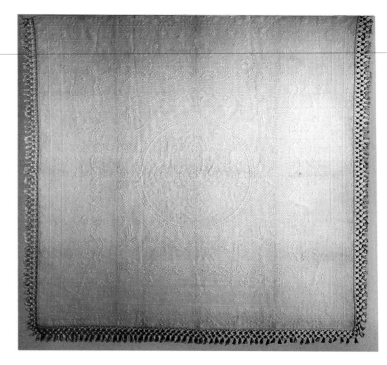

11.60.327

Counterpane, Bolton type

P A & Co.
Probably Bolton, Lancashire, England, about 1800–1830
109 × 104¼ in.
Cotton
Inscribed (looped at bottom left): *P A & Co. J2 C*
Bequest of Maria P. James, 1910

This hand-loom-woven white cotton bed cover was made in
one piece. The design is picked out in raised loops of heavy
cotton weft threads. The heavy pattern wefts are in a 1:4
proportion to the lighter-weight main wefts. The piece has a
central diamond motif surrounded by various borders and
is self-fringed on all four sides.

Reference: Montgomery 1984, p. 172.

11.60.329   (catalogue no. 47)

Quilt, Marseilles type

Maker unknown
Probably Manchester, Lancashire, England, about 1780–1820
120 × 132 in.
Cotton
Bequest of Maria P. James, 1910

This white cotton bed cover was hand-loom woven employing a technique that was designed to imitate hand quilting.
It is patterned with a central circular medallion that is
surrounded by squared borders, including one with a
pineapple in each of its four corners. It has handmade ball
fringe on three sides.

Reference: Montgomery 1984, pp. 289–92.

11.60.330

Counterpane, Bolton type

Maker unknown
Probably Bolton, Lancashire, England, about 1800–1830
122 × 113¾ in.
Cotton
Inscribed (looped at bottom left): *A S F 14*
Bequest of Maria P. James, 1910

This hand-loom-woven white cotton bed cover was made in
one piece. The design is picked out in raised loops of heavy
cotton weft threads. The heavy pattern wefts are in a 1:3
proportion to the lighter-weight main wefts. The central
design is crossed keys, and there are surrounding borders
of tulips, flowers in pots, and zigzags.

Reference: Montgomery 1984, p. 172.

17.42.2   (catalogue no. 48)

Counterpane, Bolton type

Maker unknown
Possibly New York City, about 1810–35
111½ × 105¼ in.
Cotton
Gift of Miss H. Rhoades, 1917

This hand-loom-woven white cotton bed cover was made in
one piece. The design is picked out in raised loops of heavy
cotton weft threads. The heavy pattern wefts are in a 1:6
proportion to the lighter-weight main wefts. It has a central
motif of an eagle surmounted by thirteen stars. This eagle
motif is surrounded by various floral and swag borders.
The piece is self-fringed on the left and right sides.

References: Armentrout (forthcoming); Montgomery 1984
p. 172; Schwartz 1958.

37.164

Counterpane, Bolton type

Maker unknown
Probably Bolton, Lancashire, England, about 1800–1830
101 × 89½ in.
Cotton
Inscribed (looped at bottom left): *I.S.M.S.F.*
Gift of Mrs. Courtney Brown, 1937

This hand-loom-woven white cotton bed cover was made in
one piece. The design is picked out in raised loops of heavy
cotton weft threads. The heavy pattern wefts are in a 1:2
proportion to the lighter-weight main wefts. The piece has a
central eight-pointed star motif, which is surrounded by
various borders. It is self-fringed on all four sides.

Reference: Montgomery 1984, p. 172.

42.46

Quilt, Marseilles type

Maker unknown
United States or Great Britain, about 1876
104¼ × 97 in.
Cotton
Inscribed (woven below eagle): *E PLURIBUS UNUM*
Gift of Virginia D. Lyman, 1942

This loom-woven bed cover has warps of both red and
white cotton and a weft of white cotton. It was woven to
imitate hand quilting. The central design is an eagle with
outspread wings standing above the words *E PLURIBUS
UNUM.* Thirteen stars are visible above the eagle's head.
The remaining ground is covered with floral and foliage
borders.

Reference: Montgomery 1984, pp. 289–92.

Notes: It is possible that this bed cover was woven for the
1876 Centennial. The thistle (Scotland), rose (England), and
clover (Ireland) motifs in the central areas of the top and
bottom borders may indicate that the piece was made in
Great Britain and then imported as a Centennial souvenir.
The piece is in poor condition.

47.93

Counterpane, Bolton type

Maker unknown
Probably Bolton, Lancashire, England, about 1800–1830
109¼ × 102¾ in.
Cotton
Inscribed (looped at bottom left): *T H M F12*
Gift of Mrs. Arnold Burges Johnson, 1947

This hand-loom-woven white cotton bed cover was made in
one piece. The design is picked out in raised loops of heavy
cotton weft threads. The heavy pattern wefts are in a 1:2
proportion to the lighter-weight main wefts. The small
central eight-pointed star is surrounded by various borders.
The piece is self-fringed on all four sides.

Reference: Montgomery 1984, p. 172.

1980.498.4

Quilt, Marseilles type

Maker unknown
Probably United States, about 1865
100 × 93 in.
Cotton
Gift of Mrs. Andrew Galbraith Carey, 1980

This white cotton bed cover was loom woven, using a
technique designed to imitate hand quilting. The central
medallion is surrounded by a wide border of naturalistic
roses and ferns intertwined with a Greek-key motif border.
The outer border is composed of woven diamond quilting.

Reference: Montgomery 1984, pp. 289–92.

13.207   (catalogue no. 62)

Bed Rug

Maker unknown
Probably New London County, Connecticut, 1809
102 × 99⅛ in.
Pile: wool; *foundation:* wool
Inscribed (in wool pile at top center): *M B/1809*
Rogers Fund, 1913

This bed rug is needleworked in looped running stitch, which has been cut to form a pile surface on the light brown/ochre woven wool base. The base is made of three panels of fabric, sewn together at their selvedges. The bed rug is decorated with a central pattern of branching flowers stemming from a single vase, along with a border of large flowers and twisting vines in shades of rust brown, light brown, yellow beige, and moss green with a black background.

Publications: Callister and Warren 1972, no. 34; Safford and Bishop 1972.

Notes: The bed rug shows some old repairs and is in fragile condition.

33.122   (catalogue no. 63)

Bed Rug

Maker unknown
Colchester, New London County, Connecticut, 1796
93¼ × 89 in.
Pile: wool; *foundation:* wool
Inscribed (in wool pile at top center): *1796/ Ⅶ L*
Rogers Fund, 1933

This bed rug is needleworked in a looped running stitch, which has been cut to form a pile surface on the natural-colored woven wool base. The base is made of three panels of fabric sewn together at their selvedges with one narrow piece sewn at the left side. The bed rug is decorated with a central pattern of branching flowers stemming from a single vase and has a border of flowers and twisting vines in shades of brown, gold, green, and tan on a natural cream ground.

Publications: "All Wool and Wide" 1934; Callister and Warren 1972, no. 26; Downs 1934, pp. 6–7.

Notes: Although it is in fair condition, this bed rug has been extensively repaired.

22.55 (catalogue no. 67)

Coverlet, embroidered

Mary Breed (1751–?)
Probably New London County, Connecticut, 1770
90¾ × 89 in.
Base: linen/cotton; *embroidery*: wool
Inscribed (in cross stitch at bottom center, visible in 1922):
   MARY BREED/AGE 19 Y 1770; (visible at present): *MARY
   BREED/[indecipherable]/1770*; thread marking inscription
   seems to be a 1962 replacement
Rogers Fund, 1922

The undyed linen/cotton base fabric of this coverlet is
embroidered with wool in shades of blue, gold, pink, black,
and brown. The principal stitch used is the economy stitch,
but details are embroidered in herringbone stitch, stem
stitch, buttonhole stitch, chevron-patterned darning, couch-
ing, and outline stitch. The base is made of two large center
panels and three narrow borders, which probably were
once two bed curtains and three bed valances. The embroidered design is composed of widely spaced bouquets of
flowers and birds in fruit trees. The bottom edge has been
cut to fit around bedposts.

Publications: Cornelius 1922; Harbeson 1938, p. 32; "A New
England Bedspread" 1922; Rowe 1973, pp. 144–49.

Notes: This piece was conserved in 1962, at which time it
suffered losses to its original cross-stitch inscription.

23.20.1

Coverlet, embroidered whitework

Probably Jane Simonton Chapman (1794–?)
Orange County, New York, about 1821–25
102¾ × 75½ in.
Base: cotton; *embroidery*: cotton
Inscribed (in loops under eagles): *T C 1825 / I S 1821*
Gift of Jane A. Everdell, in memory of Cornelia Augusta
    Chapman Everdell, 1923

This whitework coverlet is composed of three lengths of
twill-weave fabric stitched together. It is embroidered with
loops of heavy white cotton thread, sometimes called "candlewicking." A large eight-pointed star is embroidered in
the center with an eagle above it and one beneath it. The
central motifs are surrounded by flowering potted plants
and a swag border. The coverlet is fringed on all four sides;
each piece of fringe is drawn through the hem individually.

Notes: This coverlet appears to be a hand-embroidered copy
of a Bolton counterpane. It came to the Museum along with
a number of items supposedly made by the donor's mater-
nal grandmother, Jane Simonton. Included in the lot is a
sampler dated 1808 and signed by Jane Simonton, aged
fourteen. Simonton must have married a Mr. Chapman,
since the donor's mother, Cornelia Augusta Chapman Everdell, in whose memory the piece was given, had the maiden
name of Chapman. Perhaps the inscription *T C* on the
coverlet stands for Mr. Chapman. The other inscription on
the coverlet is a barred *I S*, perhaps for Jane Simonton. The
barred *I* and the letter *J* were used interchangeably throughout the eighteenth century, and Simonton could have been
using this older form, especially since she did use the
barred *I* for *J* on her 1808 sampler. Unfortunately, we do not
know the significance of the two dates on the coverlet. In
addition to her sampler, the Museum also owns a pillow-
case marked with barred *I S* that may have been from Jane
Simonton's trousseau.

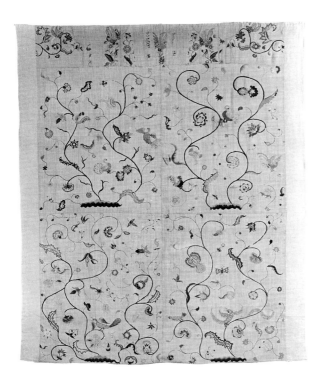

24.188

Coverlet, embroidered

Maker unknown
England or America, about 1720
83½ × 69½ in.
Base: linen; *embroidery*: wool
The Sylmaris Collection, Gift of George Coe Graves, 1924

This linen coverlet is embroidered with multicolored wools in satin stitch, long and short stitch, buttonhole stitch, stem stitch, and a variety of filling stitches. It is composed of four panels, each about 37 × 30 inches, with a band of twelve small pieces stitched together along the top. Each large panel is embroidered with flowering trees of life, upon which birds are perched. The piece is backed and bordered by new, machine-stitched linen.

Notes: This piece was not always a coverlet. The top strip is fabricated out of small shaped pieces that could be either bits of a valance or the bodice of a dress. The larger panels may have been window curtains, but their size and decoration make it more likely that they were the skirt panels of an eighteenth-century gown. Although the coverlet came to the Museum in 1924 with an American attribution, the unusual sophistication of the embroidered motifs and the elaborate nature of the needlework, which lacks the self-couching and economy stitches typically found in American work, make an English attribution more probable.

L.1925 (catalogue no. 64)

Blanket, embroidered

Henriet Tyler
Connecticut River Valley area, Connecticut or
 Massachusetts, 1822
87 × 88½ in.
Base: wool; *embroidery*: wool
Inscribed (embroidered at top in oblong floral wreath):
 Henriet Tyler. 1822
Lent by Elizabeth Ward

Three panels of black wool fabric, each approximately 28½ inches wide, are stitched together to form the base of this blanket. It is embroidered with green, blue, yellow, and orange wool, using back stitch, cross stitch, buttonhole stitch, satin stitch, and French knots. A separately woven dark blue wool fringe is attached on three sides. The pattern (beginning at the center) is of large curling floral vines, a swag-and-tassel inner border, and a row of paisley shapes making up the outer border.

References: Callister and Warren 1972; "Embroidered Wool Coverlets" 1940; H.E.K. 1932; "Wool-on-Wool Coverlets" 1938.

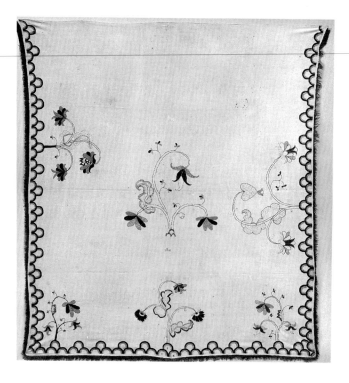

27.242

Coverlet, embroidered whitework

Mercy Emerson Tomlinson
Kentucky, about 1820
102 × 85¾ in.
Base: cotton; *embroidery*: cotton
Gift of Cora Parker, in memory of her mother, Pamela Ann
    Parker, 1927

This whitework coverlet is made of three lengths of white
cotton fabric that have been stitched together. Some of the
decorated areas are tufted, and others are embroidered
with heavy white cotton thread in satin stitch. The pattern
consists of an overall floral vine. The piece is fringed on all
four sides.

Notes: The fringe on this piece is particularly interesting.
On two sides, there is a heavy loom-woven openwork,
while on the remaining two sides the fringe is of a rather
delicate hand-knitted type. Both fringes seem to be original
to the piece. Perhaps Tomlinson tired of knitting and decided to finish the piece with a woven fringe, which is
quicker to make.

28.96

Blanket, embroidered

Ruth Brewster Sampson
Massachusetts, 1801
95½ × 84¼ in.
Base: wool; *embroidery*: wool
Inscribed (embroidered in cross stitch): *1801/S/S R*
Rogers Fund, 1928

The cream-colored wool ground of this bed cover is embroidered with light and dark blue wool in flat stitch, chain
stitch, outline stitch, and small dotlike running stitches. The
central area is decorated with six small flowering trees. The
border is in a "hillock" pattern. The wool ground is made
up of three panels seamed together. There is a dark blue
wool fringe on three sides.

Publication: F. L. 1928, p. 206.

Notes: When the Museum purchased this bed cover in 1928,
we were told that it was spun, woven, and embroidered by
Ruth Brewster, the great-great-great-granddaughter of Elder
Brewster. Ruth married Samuel Sampson, and after her
death, Samuel was cared for by Deborah Butts Day, the
great-grandmother of the blanket's owner. At Samuel
Sampson's death, the work was willed to Deborah Butts
Day, who lived in South Hadley Falls, Massachusetts. The
initials embroidered at the bottom of the piece are assumed
to stand for Samuel and Ruth Sampson.

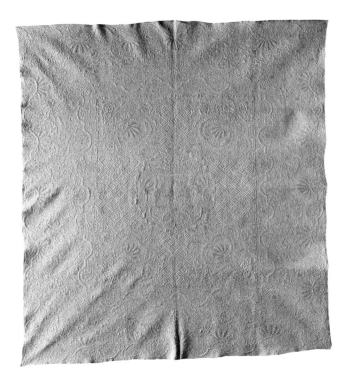

35.44

Quilt, embroidered and stuffed whitework

Maker unknown
England, about 1720
104¼ × 92¾ in.
Base: linen; *embroidery:* linen; *binding:* linen (new); *filling:* wool
Rogers Fund, 1935

This whitework bed cover is decorated with both quilting and surface embroidery. The central ground is quilted in a basket weave pattern, with a floral medallion in the middle and shell motifs at each corner. The wide border of floral and shell motifs is surrounded by quilted strapwork. The piece is embroidered in a variety of stitches, and in some areas the linen embroidery threads have been woven over and under each other to make lacelike designs over the surface of the quilt.

Publication: Downs 1928, p. 180.

Notes: Although according to our records this bed cover came from a house in Middletown, Connecticut, it is unlikely that it was made in America. The remarkable intricacies of the design and the high quality of the stitching lead to the conclusion that it was made by a professional embroiderer in England and may have come to America with an immigrating family. The few documented American coverlets from the early 1700s lack the sophistication and fine craftsmanship of this piece.

39.111   (catalogue no. 70)

Coverlet, embroidered whitework

Mary Walker Stith Jones (1802–1884)
Breckinridge County, Kentucky, about 1815–18
100½ × 87¼ in.
Base: cotton; *embroidery:* cotton
Inscribed (embroidered at bottom left corner): J
Fletcher Fund, 1939

Made of three lengths of cotton seamed together, this whitework coverlet is embroidered with heavy cotton thread in many different stitches. Some areas are decorated with drawnwork. The central design is a basket of flowers within a diamond-shaped medallion. The remaining ground is decorated with meandering floral vines. There is a woven fringe on three sides.

41.183   (catalogue no. 65)

Blanket, embroidered

Maker unknown
New York or New England, about 1835
79 × 71 in.
Base: wool; *embroidery*: cotton
Rogers Fund, 1941

The dark blue twill-woven ground of this blanket is embroidered in heavy white cotton thread with economy stitches and stem stitches. The central area is decorated with large medallions. Three sides are bordered with embroidered vines, and the top edge has small embroidered leaves. The piece is made of two panels of fabric, which have been seamed at the center.

44.140   (catalogue no. 66)

Bed Curtain, embroidered

Sarah Noyes Chester (1722–1797)
Wethersfield, Hartford County, Connecticut, about 1745
87¾ × 70⅝ in.
Base: linen; *embroidery*: wool
Gift of Mr. and Mrs. Frank Coit Johnson, through their sons
    and daughter, 1944

This piece is made of three panels of linen stitched together and embroidered with wool in satin, split, stem, star, and French-knot stitches. It is embroidered through two layers of linen, the top layer of which is extremely fine. It has been rebacked since it came to the Museum. The central area is embroidered with fruit trees and flowering plants, including pear, yellow apple, cherry, thistle, carnation, and rose. The piece is bordered on three sides with fantastic flowering vines in shades of blue, green, yellow, salmon, pink, and red.

Publications: Jeffrey 1945, pp. 120–22; Rowe 1973, fig. 30;
Safford and Bishop 1972, fig. 40.
Reference: Watkins 1976.

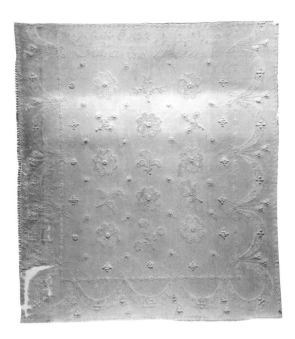

46.125

Coverlet, embroidered whitework

Catharine Woolsey (1775–?)
Dutchess County, New York, 1822
96½ × 85¼ in.
Base: cotton; *embroidery:* cotton
Inscribed (embroidered at top): *Nov 27th 1822 hand/Catharine Woolsey's*
Rogers Fund, 1946

This whitework coverlet is made of two panels of ribbed cotton that are seamed at the center. It is embroidered with heavy white cotton thread in stem, back, and running stitches, French knots, and tufting. The central ground is embroidered with equally spaced flowers and floral sprigs, and there is a swag-and-tassel border. The piece is fringed on three sides.

Notes: Catharine Woolsey was the descendant of an English family that was exiled to Holland in 1610 and came to New York in 1623 with the first Dutch immigrants. The family became successful merchants and owned a business that continued to be run by successive generations. Catharine Woolsey's grandfather Benjamin (born 1717) brought the family to Dutchess County. The daughter of Samuel Woolsey (born March 20, 1745) and Mary Knickerbocker Gillette (born June 24, 1747), Catharine Woolsey was one of ten children and the great-aunt of the person who sold the coverlet to the Museum. Unfortunately, the coverlet is in very deteriorated condition.

49.119

Coverlet, embroidered whitework

Prudence Clark
United States, 1817
101½ × 91¾ in.
Base: linen/cotton; *embroidery:* cotton
Inscribed (embroidered at top): *Prudence Clark/1817*
Gift of Juliet Evelyn Hitchcock, 1949

Three panels of a linen/cotton ribbed fabric are seamed together to form the base of this whitework coverlet. The piece is embroidered in loops with heavy white cotton thread. The central medallion is set within an octagon of interlocking rings, which in turn is surrounded by two abstract floral borders.

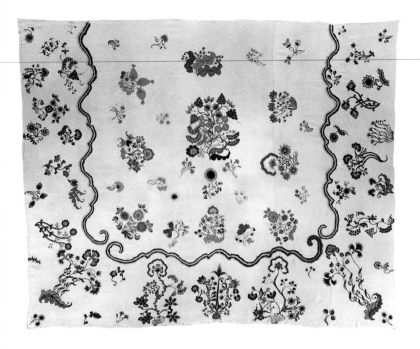

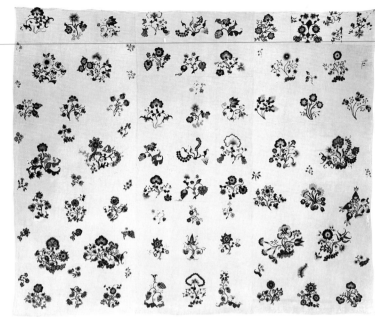

61.48.1   (catalogue no. 68)

Coverlet, embroidered

Ruth Culver Coleman
Possibly Sag Harbor, Suffolk County, New York, about
   1760–75
80¾ × 95⅝ in.
Base: linen; *embroidery*: wool
Sansbury-Mills Fund, 1961

The coverlet is composed of three undyed linen panels
seamed together, each approximately thirty-two inches
wide. It is embroidered with wool in economy, stem, chain,
and darning stitches. The wide floral border is embroidered
in shades of blue; the central floral and fruit motifs are in
shades of pink, brown, gold, lavender, and blue. The top
edge of the coverlet seems to have been cut off.

Publications: Howe 1976, pp. 128–36; The Metropolitan
Museum of Art (exhib. cat.) 1909, no. 592.

61.48.2   (catalogue no. 69)

Bed Hangings, embroidered

Ruth Culver Coleman
Possibly Sag Harbor, Suffolk County, New York, about
   1760–75
85 × 99 in.
Base: linen and linen/cotton; *embroidery*: wool
Sansbury-Mills Fund, 1961

This work is composed of nine different-size panels of
embroidered fabric; some panels are woven exclusively of
linen, and others are of a linen/cotton fabric. The piece is
embroidered with the same stitches as 61.48.1 in floral
motifs in multiple shades of blue wool.

Publications: Howe 1976, pp. 128–36; The Metropolitan
Museum of Art (exhib. cat.) 1909, no. 592.

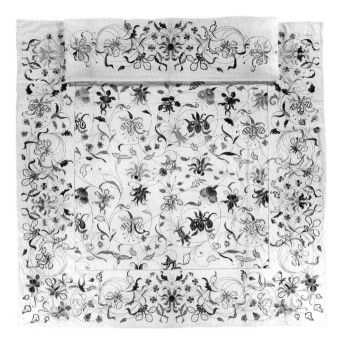

65.238

Coverlet, embroidered whitework

Ann (or Nancy) Elliott Grigg (1795–1839)
Rutherford County, North Carolina, about 1810–15
83⅝ × 90 in.
Base: cotton; *embroidery:* cotton
Inscribed (woven in fringe): *NANCY ELLIOTT ANN
 ELLIOTT ANN ELLIOTT ANN ELLIOTT N*
Gift of Mrs. William K. Dupre, 1965

This whitework coverlet is made of three panels of woven cotton fabric that have been seamed together. It is embroidered with heavy white cotton thread in a variety of stitches and includes areas of drawnwork. The piece is decorated with a central basket with a flowering tree and birds, which is surrounded by a ribbon border and a wide outer border of vines and flowers. The fringe is a recent reproduction of the original.

Notes: According to family history, this coverlet was made at the Elliott farm in Rutherford County, North Carolina. The cotton was grown, spun, and woven on the farm. The coverlet was made by Ann (nicknamed Nancy) Elliott, the eighth child of Martin and Nancy Finch Elliott. She was born in 1795 in Virginia; in 1802, her father moved the family and one hundred slaves to North Carolina. She married Paschal P. Grigg on March 3, 1830, at the age of thirty-five and had at least one child, a daughter named Roxanna. She died on November 11, 1839, and the coverlet was given to Roxanna, from whom it was passed down through the family until it was given to the Museum in 1965.

1986.333.1,2   (catalogue no. 71)

Coverlet and Pillow Sham, embroidered

A. P. Lalkers (?)
United States, 1898
86⅞ × 88 in.
Base: linen; *embroidery:* silk; *backing:* cotton
Inscribed (stitched in blue thread at top right): *A. P. Lalkers/
 1898* (only holes remain for date, which was intentionally
 picked out by a previous owner)
Purchase, Mrs. Roger Brunschwig Gift, 1986

The undyed linen base of this coverlet is embroidered with silk in shades of green, gold, salmon, and blue in stem and satin stitches. It is decorated with Art Nouveau–style irises and vines, following a pattern printed in blue on the linen. It is seamed at the center and backed with undyed cotton fabric.

References: Brainerd and Armstrong Company 1899; Garrett 1876; Harrison 1881; Lockwood and Glaister 1878; "Quilts and Coverlets" 1881.

Bibliography

Affleck, Diane L. Fagan. *Just New From the Mills: Printed Cottons in America, Late Nineteenth and Early Twentieth Centuries.* North Andover, Mass.: Museum of American Textile History, 1987.

"All Wool and Wide." *Antiques* 26 (Nov. 1934), pp. 168–69.

Allen, Gloria Seaman. "Jacquard Coverlets in the D.A.R. Museum, Part I: New York Coverlets." *Antiques* 127 (Jan. 1985), pp. 292–99.

———. "Jacquard Coverlets in the D.A.R. Museum, Part II: Pennsylvania Coverlets." *Antiques* 130 (July 1986), pp. 132–39.

———. *First Flowerings: Early Virginia Quilts.* Washington, D.C.: Daughters of the American Revolution Museum, 1987.

Anderson, Mary. "Her Storybook Quilts Are a Hit." *New York World-Telegram*, 26 Jan. 1944.

Armentrout, Sandra S. "Eliza Bourne of Kennebunk: Professional Fancy Weaver, 1800–1820." *House and Home.* Annual Proceedings of the Dublin Seminar for New England Folk Life, 1988. Boston: Boston University Press, forthcoming.

Atwater, Mary Meigs. *The Shuttle-Craft Book of American Hand-Weaving.* New York: Macmillan, 1928. Rev. ed., 1951.

Bacon, Lenice Ingram. *American Patchwork Quilts.* New York: William Morrow, 1973.

The Baltimore Museum of Art. *The Great American Cover-Up: Counterpanes of the Eighteenth and Nineteenth Centuries.* Baltimore, Md.: Baltimore Museum of Art, 1971.

Beecher, Catherine E., and Stowe, Harriet Beecher. *The American Woman's Home; Or: Principles of Domestic Science.* New York: J. B. Ford, 1869. Repr., Hartford, Conn.: Stowe-Day Foundation, 1987.

Beer, Alice Baldwin. *Trade Goods: A Study of Indian Chintz in the Collection of the Cooper-Hewitt Museum.* Washington, D.C.: Smithsonian Institution, 1970.

Benberry, Cuesta. "Quilt Cottage Industries: A Chronicle." *Uncoverings* 7 (1986), pp. 83–100.

Betterton, Shiela. *Quilts and Coverlets from The American Museum in Britain.* Bath: American Museum in Britain, 1978. Repr., 1982.

———. *More Quilts and Coverlets from The American Museum in Britain.* Bath: American Museum in Britain, 1989.

Binney, Edwin, 3rd, and Binney-Winslow, Gail. *Homage to Amanda: Two Hundred Years of American Quilts.* San Francisco: R. K. Press, 1984.

The Birmingham Museum of Art. *Black Belt to Hill Country: Alabama Quilts from the Robert and Helen Cargo Collection.* Birmingham, Ala.: Birmingham Museum of Art, 1981.

Bishop, Robert, and Coblentz, Patricia. *New Discoveries in American Quilts.* New York: E. P. Dutton, 1975.

Bishop, Robert, and Safanda, Elizabeth. *A Gallery of Amish Quilts: Design Diversity from a Plain People.* New York: E. P. Dutton, 1976.

Blauvelt, Louis L. *The Blauvelt Family Genealogy.* Blauvelt, N.Y.: The Association of Blauvelt Descendants, 1957.

Blum, Dilys, and Lindsey, Jack L. "Nineteenth Century Appliqué Quilts." *Philadelphia Museum of Art Bulletin* 85 (Fall 1989).

Bordes, Marilynn Johnson. *12 Great Quilts from the American Wing.* New York: The Metropolitan Museum of Art, 1974.

Brainerd and Armstrong Company. *Embroidery Lessons.* New London, Conn.: Brainerd and Armstrong Company, 1899.

Brockett, Linus Pierpont. *The Silk Industry in America: A History, Prepared for the Centennial Exposition.* New York: Silk Association of America, 1876.

Burke, Doreen Bolger, et al. *In Pursuit of Beauty.* New York: The Metropolitan Museum of Art and Rizzoli, 1986.

Burnham, Dorothy K. *Warp and Weft: A Dictionary of Textile Terms.* Toronto: Royal Ontario Museum, 1980; New York: Charles Scribner's Sons, 1981.

Burnham, Harold B. and Dorothy K. *"Keep me warm one night": Early Handweaving in Eastern Canada.* Toronto: University of Toronto Press and Royal Ontario Museum, 1972.

Callister, J. Herbert, and Warren, William L. *Bed Ruggs/ 1722–1833.* Hartford, Conn.: Wadsworth Atheneum, 1972.

Carlisle, Lilian Baker. *Pieced Work and Appliqué Quilts at Shelburne Museum.* Museum Pamphlet Series, no. 2. Shelburne, Vt.: Shelburne Museum, 1957.

The Carpet Trade and Review 16, no. 7 (April 1885).

Caulfeild, Sophia Frances Anne, and Saward, Blanche C. *The Dictionary of Needlework: An Encyclopaedia of Artistic, Plain, and Fancy Needlework.* London: L. Upcott Gill, 1882. Facsimile ed., New York: Arno Press, 1972.

Cavallo, Adolph S. *Needlework.* New York: Cooper-Hewitt Museum, 1979.

Chapman, Etta Tyler. "The Tyler Coverlets." *Antiques* 13 (March 1928), pp. 215–18.

Cincinnati Art Museum. *Quilts from Cincinnati Collections.* Cincinnati: Cincinnati Art Museum, 1985.

Clarke, Mary Washington. *Kentucky Quilts and Their Makers.* Lexington, Ky.: University Press of Kentucky, 1976.

Colby, Averil. *Patchwork.* London: B. T. Batsford, 1958.

———. *Patchwork Quilts.* New York: Charles Scribner's Sons, 1965.

———. *Quilting.* New York: Charles Scribner's Sons, 1971.

Collins, Herbert Ridgeway. *Threads of History: Americana Recorded on Cloth, 1775 to the Present.* Washington, D.C.: Smithsonian Institution, 1979.

Colonial Coverlet Guild of America. *Heirlooms from Old Looms: A Catalogue of Coverlets Owned by the Colonial Coverlet Guild of America and Its Members*. Chicago: Priv. print., 1940.

Cooper, Grace Rogers. *The Copp Family Textiles*. Washington, D.C.: Smithsonian Institution, 1971.

Cornelius, Charles Over. "The Museum and the Collector." *Antiques* 1 (May 1922), pp. 230–31.

Cowdin, Elliot C. *Report to the Department of State on Silk and Silk Manufactures*. Washington, D.C., 1868.

Craft and Folk Art Museum. *Nineteenth Century American Coverlets*. Los Angeles: Craft and Folk Art Museum, 1976.

Cummings, Abbott Lowell, comp. *Bed Hangings: A Treatise on Fabrics and Styles in the Curtaining of Beds 1650–1850*. Boston: Society for the Preservation of New England Antiquities, 1961.

Curtis, Phillip H. "American Quilts in the Newark Museum Collection." *The Museum* 25 (Summer–Fall 1973), pp. 2–68.

Davis, Mildred J. *Early American Embroidery Designs*. New York: Crown Publishers, 1969.

Davison, Mildred. *American Quilts from The Art Institute of Chicago*. Chicago: Art Institute of Chicago, 1966.

———. "Five Related Coverlets." *Antiques* 102 (Oct. 1972), pp. 650–52.

Davison, Mildred and Mayer-Thurman, Christa C. *Coverlets: A Handbook on the Collection of Woven Coverlets in The Art Institute of Chicago*. Chicago: Art Institute of Chicago, 1973.

DeGraw, Imelda G. *Quilts and Coverlets*. Denver: Denver Art Museum, 1974.

Downs, Joseph. "An American Rug." *Bulletin of The Metropolitan Museum of Art* 29 (Jan. 1934), pp. 6–7.

———. "Four American Coverlets." *Bulletin of The Metropolitan Museum of Art* 33 (Aug. 1938), pp. 180–82.

Dunton, William Rush, Jr. *Old Quilts*. Catonsville, Md.: Publ. by the author, 1946.

Elvehjem Art Center. *American Coverlets of the Nineteenth Century from the Helen Louise Allen Textile Collection*. Madison, Wis.: University of Wisconsin, 1974.

"Embroidered Wool Coverlets." *Antiques* 37 (Feb. 1940), p. 63.

F. L. "An American Embroidered Coverlet." *Bulletin of The Metropolitan Museum of Art* 23 (Aug. 1928), p. 206.

Ferrero, Pat; Hedges, Elaine; and Silber, Julie. *Hearts and Hands: The Influence of Women and Quilts on American Society*. San Francisco: Quilt Digest Press, 1987.

Finley, Ruth E. *Old Patchwork Quilts and the Women Who Made Them*. Philadelphia and London: J. B. Lippincott, 1929.

Floud, Peter. "Design Review: A Calendar of English Furnishing Textiles: 1775–1905." *Architectural Review* 120 (Aug. 1956), pp. 126–33.

Fox, Sandi. *Quilts in Utah: A Reflection of the Western Experience*. Salt Lake City: Salt Lake Art Center, 1981.

Garrett, Rhoda and Agnes. *Suggestions for House Decoration in Painting, Woodwork and Furniture*. London: Macmillan, 1876.

Godey's Lady's Book [Philadelphia]. 1830–98 [1830–48: *Lady's Book*].

Gunn, Virginia. "Template Quilt Construction and Its Offshoots." In *Pieced by Mother: Over 100 Years of Quiltmaking Traditions*. Lewisburg, Pa.: Oral Traditions Project of the Union County Historical Society, 1987.

H. E. K. "Embroidered Coverlets." *Antiques* 22 (Dec. 1932), pp. 229–30.

Haders, Phyllis. *Sunshine and Shadow: The Amish and Their Quilts*. Pittstown, N.J.: Main Street Press, 1984. Origin. publ. New York: Universe Books, 1976.

Hall, Carrie A., and Kretzinger, Rose G. *The Romance of the Patchwork Quilt in America*. Caldwell, Idaho: Caxton Printers, 1935. Repr., New York: Dover, 1988.

Hall, Eliza Calvert. *A Book of Hand-Woven Coverlets*. Boston: Little, Brown, 1912.

Harbeson, Georgiana Brown. *American Needlework: The History of Decorative Stitchery and Embroidery from the Late 16th to the 20th Century*. New York: Coward-McCann, 1938.

Harrison, Constance Cary. *Woman's Handiwork in Modern Homes*. New York: Charles Scribner's Sons, 1881.

Heisey, John W., comp. *A Checklist of American Coverlet Weavers*. Williamsburg, Va.: Colonial Williamsburg Foundation, 1978.

Herr, Patricia T. "All in Modesty and Plainness." *The Quilt Digest* 3 (1985), pp. 22–35.

———. "Quaker Quilts and Their Makers." In *Pieced by Mother: Over 100 Years of Quiltmaking Traditions*. Lewisburg, Pa.: Oral Traditions Project of the Union County Historical Society, 1987.

Hoke, Donald, comp. *Dressing the Bed: Quilts and Coverlets from the Collections of The Milwaukee Public Museum*. Milwaukee, Wis.: Milwaukee Public Museum, 1985.

Holstein, Jonathan. *The Pieced Quilt: An American Design Tradition*. Greenwich, Conn.: New York Graphic Society, 1973.

"Hope Deferred." *Antiques* 42 (Dec. 1942), p. 312.

Howe, Florence Thompson. "Three Stenciled Counterpanes." *Antiques* 37 (March 1940), pp. 120–22.

Howe, Margery Burnham. *Deerfield Embroidery*. New York: Charles Scribner's Sons, 1976. Repr. Deerfield, Mass.: Pocumtuck Valley Memorial Association, 1983.

Ickis, Marguerite. *The Standard Book of Quilt Making and Collecting*. New York: Dover, 1959; repr. of Greystone Press, 1949.

Irwin, John Rice. *A People and Their Quilts*. Exton, Pa.: Schiffer Publishing, 1983.

Jeffrey, Margaret. "Early American Embroidery." *Metropolitan Museum of Art Bulletin* 3 (Jan. 1945), pp. 120–25.

Katzenberg, Dena S. *Baltimore Album Quilts*. Baltimore, Md.: Baltimore Museum of Art, 1981.

Khin, Yvonne M. *The Collector's Dictionary of Quilt Names and Patterns*. Washington, D.C.: Acropolis Books, 1980.

Kobayashi, Kei, ed. *Shelburne Museum: The Quilt*. Tokyo: Gakken, 1985.

Lasansky, Jeanette. *In the Heart of Pennsylvania: 19th and 20th Century Quiltmaking Traditions*. Lewisburg, Pa.:

Oral Traditions Project of the Union County Historical Society, 1985.

———. *Pieced by Mother: Over 100 Years of Quiltmaking
Traditions*. Lewisburg, Pa.: Oral Traditions Project of
the Union County Historical Society, 1987.

Lasansky, Jeanette, et al. *In the Heart of Pennsylvania:
Symposium Papers*. Lewisburg, Pa.: Oral Traditions
Project of the Union County Historical Society, 1986.

———. *Pieced by Mother: Symposium Papers*. Lewisburg,
Pa.: Oral Traditions Project of the Union County
Historical Society, 1988.

Leslie, Eliza. *The Girl's Own Book* [also *American Girl's
Book*] *: Or, Occupation for Play Hours*. Boston: DeWolfe,
Fiske, n.d.

Lipsett, Linda Otto. *Remember Me: Women and Their
Friendship Quilts*. San Francisco: Quilt Digest Press,
1985.

Little, Frances. *Early American Textiles*. New York: Century Company, 1931.

"Little-known Masterpieces, II: An Eighteenth Century
Patchwork Quilt." *Antiques* 1 (Feb. 1922), pp. 67–68.

Lockwood, M. S., and Glaister, E. *Art Embroidery: A
Treatise on the Revived Practice of Decorative Needlework*.
London: Marcus Ward, 1878.

Logan, Mrs. John A. *The Home Manual*. Philadelphia,
1889.

Martin, George A. *Our Homes; How to Beautify Them*.
New York: Judd Co., 1888.

McMorris, Penny. *Crazy Quilts*. New York: E. P. Dutton,
1984.

McMorris, Penny, and Kile, Michael. *The Art Quilt*. San
Francisco: Quilt Digest Press, 1986.

Metropolitan Art Series. *Needle and Brush: Useful and
Decorative*. New York: Butterick Publishing Company,
1889.

———. *Needle-Craft: Artistic and Practical*. New York:
Butterick Publishing Company, 1890.

The Metropolitan Museum of Art. *The Hudson-Fulton
Celebration*. Vol. 2. New York: The Metropolitan Museum of Art, 1909.

Montgomery, Florence M. *Printed Textiles: English and
American Cottons and Linens 1700–1850*. New York:
Viking Press, 1970.

———. *Textiles in America, 1650–1870*. New York: W. W.
Norton, 1984.

Moss, Gillian. "David D. Haring and Bergen County
Coverlets." *Relics: The Newsletter of the Pascack Historical Society* 19 (March 1975), pp. 2–4.

———. *Printed Textiles, 1760–1860, in the Collection of the
Cooper-Hewitt Museum*. Washington, D.C.: Smithsonian
Institution, 1987.

Murray, Anne Wood. "The Attitude of the Eagle, As
Portrayed on an Outstanding Group of 'Liberty'
Quilts." *Antiques* 52 (July 1947), pp. 28–30.

Nebraska University/Sheldon Memorial Art Gallery. *Quilts
from Nebraska Collections*. Lincoln, Neb.: Mid-America
Arts Alliance, 1974.

"A New England Bedspread." *Bulletin of The Metropolitan
Museum of Art* 17 (May 1922), p. 116.

The New-York Historical Society. *American Scenes and
Events on Textiles: An Exhibition of Printed Cottons,
Linens, and Silks from 1777–1941*. New York: New-
York Historical Society, 1941.

Nicoll, Jessica F. *Quilted for Friends: Delaware Valley Signature Quilts, 1840–1855*. Winterthur, Del.: Henry Francis DuPont Winterthur Museum, 1986.

Orlofsky, Patsy and Myron. *Quilts in America*. New York:
McGraw-Hill, 1974.

Osaki, Amy Boyce. "A 'Truly Feminine Employment':
Sewing and the Early Nineteenth-Century Woman."
Winterthur Portfolio 23, no. 4 (Winter 1988), pp. 225–41.

Oshins, Lisa Turner. *Quilt Collections: A Directory for the
United States and Canada*. Washington, D.C.: Acropolis Books, 1987.

Parslow, Virginia D. "James Alexander, Weaver." *Antiques*
69 (April 1956), pp. 346–49.

"A Patriotic Quilt." *Antiques* 35 (June 1939), p. 304.

Peck, Amelia. Entry. *Recent Acquisitions, 1987–1988*. New
York: The Metropolitan Museum of Art, 1988, p. 59.

———. Entries. *Recent Acquisitions, 1988–1989*. New York:
The Metropolitan Museum of Art, 1989, pp. 60–61.

Peck, Jessie Farrall. "Weavers of New York's Historical
Coverlets." *Antiques* 18 (July 1930), pp. 22–25.

Pellman, Rachel and Kenneth. *The World of Amish Quilts*.
Intercourse, Pa.: Good Books, 1984.

Peto, Florence. "Quilts and Coverlets from New York
and Long Island." *Antiques* 33 (May 1938), pp. 265–67.

———. *Historic Quilts*. New York: American Historical
Company, 1939.

———. "New York Quilts." *New York History* 30 (July
1949), pp. 328–39.

Philadelphia Museum of Art and The Henry Francis
DuPont Winterthur Museum. *Pennsylvania German
Art 1683–1850*. Chicago and London: University of
Chicago Press, 1984.

Pottinger, David. *Quilts from the Indiana Amish: A Regional
Collection*. New York: E. P. Dutton, 1983.

The Quilt Digest [San Francisco]. Vols. 1–5 (1983–87).

"Quilts and Coverlets." *Antiques* 87 (March 1965), pp.
327–29.

"Quilts and Coverlets." *The Art Amateur* 3/4 (March
1881), pp. 80–81.

Rae, Janet. *The Quilts of the British Isles*. New York: E. P.
Dutton, 1987.

*Records of the First Reformed Church, Fishkill, Dutchess
County, New York* and *The First Reformed Church, Hopewell, Dutchess County, New York*. Copied, typed, and
indexed by Mrs. Jean D. Worden, copyright 1981.

Roberson, Ruth Haislip, ed. *North Carolina Quilts*. Chapel
Hill, N.C.: University of North Carolina Press, 1988.

Robertson, Elizabeth Wells. *American Quilts*. New York:
Studio Publications, 1948.

Rodriguez Roque, Oswaldo. Entry. *Notable Acquisitions,
1983–1984*. New York: The Metropolitan Museum of
Art, 1984, pp. 90–91.

Rowe, Ann Pollard. "Crewel Embroidered Bed Hangings in Old and New England." *Bulletin: Museum of
Fine Arts, Boston* 71, nos. 365–66 (1973).

Safford, Carleton L., and Bishop, Robert. *America's Quilts and Coverlets*. New York: E. P. Dutton, 1972.

Sater, Joel. *The Patchwork Quilt*. Ephrata, Pa.: Science Press, 1981.

Schwartz, Esther I. "Notes from a New Jersey Collector." *Antiques* 74 (Oct. 1958), pp. 329–32.

Sexton, Carlie. *Old Fashioned Quilts*. Wheaton, Ill.: Publ. by the author, 1928.

Shaeffer, Margaret W. M.; Partridge, Virginia Parslow; and Adrosko, Rita J. *Made in New York State: Handwoven Coverlets 1820–1860*. Watertown, N.Y.: Jefferson County Historical Society, 1985.

Silber, Julie. *The Esprit Quilt Collection*. San Francisco: Esprit De Corp., 1985.

Stockton, Frank R. and Marion. *The Home: Where It Should Be And What To Put In It*. New York: G. P. Putnam & Sons, 1873.

Swan, Susan Burrows. *A Winterthur Guide to American Needlework*. New York: Crown Publishers, 1976.

———. *Plain and Fancy: American Women and Their Needlework, 1700–1850*. New York: Holt, Rinehart and Winston, 1977.

Swank, Scott T., et al. *Arts of the Pennsylvania Germans*. New York: W. W. Norton and Toronto: George McLeod, 1983.

Uncoverings. The research papers of the American Quilt Study Group [San Francisco]. Vols. 1–9 (1980–89).

Ventre, Melinda. *Warm and Wonderful: The Jacquard Coverlet*. New York: Hirschl and Adler Folk, 1988.

The Victoria and Albert Museum. *Notes on Quilting*. London: Her Majesty's Stationery Office, 1934.

———. *Notes on Applied Work and Patchwork*. London: Her Majesty's Stationery Office, 1938.

———. *Catalogue of an Exhibition of English Chintz: Two Centuries of Changing Taste*. London: Victoria and Albert Museum, 1955.

———. *Catalogue of a Loan Exhibition of English Chintz*. London: Victoria and Albert Museum, 1960.

———. *English Printed Textiles 1720–1836*. London: Her Majesty's Stationery Office, 1960.

Wadsworth Atheneum. *The Great River: Art and Society of the Connecticut Valley, 1635–1820*. Hartford, Conn., 1985.

Walker, Sandra Rambo. *Country Cloth to Coverlets: Textile Traditions in 19th Century Central Pennsylvania*. Lewisburg, Pa.: Oral Traditions Project of the Union County Historical Society, 1981.

Watkins, Susan Finlay. "Connecticut Needlework in the Webb-Deane-Stevens Museum." *Antiques* 109 (March 1976), pp. 530–44.

"Weavers of Bergen County." In Schmelz, Betty, et al. *The Tree of Life*. River Edge, N.J.: Bergen County Historical Society (1983), pp. 8–29.

Webster, Marie D. *Quilts: Their Story and How to Make Them*. Garden City: N.Y.: Tudor Publishing, 1948.

Webster, Thomas, and Parkes, Mrs. *Encyclopedia of Domestic Economy*. New York: Harper and Brothers, 1845.

White, Margaret E. *American Handwoven Coverlets in the Newark Museum*. Newark, N. J.: Newark Museum, 1947.

Winchester, Alice. "Stenciled Coverlets." *Antiques* 48 (Sept. 1945), p. 145.

Woodard, Thomas K., and Greenstein, Blanche. *Twentieth Century Quilts 1900–1950*. New York: E. P. Dutton, 1988.

"Wool-on-Wool Coverlets." *Antiques* 34 (Sept. 1938), pp. 124–25.

Index

Page numbers are in roman type. Numbers in *italics* indicate illustrations. The seventy-one Highlights of the Collection and their catalogue numbers are in **boldface**.